Newman Hall

Pilgrim Songs in Cloud and Sunshine

Newman Hall

Pilgrim Songs in Cloud and Sunshine

ISBN/EAN: 9783337293819

Printed in Europe, USA, Canada, Australia, Japan

Cover: Foto ©Thomas Meinert / pixelio.de

More available books at **www.hansebooks.com**

PILGRIM SONGS

Cloud and Sunshine.

BY

NEWMAN HALL, LL.B.

LONDON:

HAMILTON, ADAMS & CO.,

PATERNOSTER ROW.

DEDICATORY SONNET.

TO MY MOTHER.

MOTHER! to thee, of right, this book belongs;
For, seated on thy knee, an infant weak,
With lisping tongue, I learnt from thee to speak,
" In psalms, and hymns, and spiritual songs."
Oft didst thou stroke my head, and kiss my cheek,
And weep for joy, to hear thy child repeat
How the good Shepherd came from heaven, to seek
His wandering lambs,—and how His hands and feet
Were pierced with nails—while He, the sufferer meek,
Prayed for his foes, then mounted to His throne.
With themes like these, my years have still upgrown,
Through thy persuasive teaching, tender care,
Thine, and a loving father's life of prayer.
The book I offer thee is thus thine own !

PREFATORY SONNET.

A THOUSAND seeds are formed, for one to root ;
Of many arrows, few quite reach the mark ;
Of many blows, few strike the kindling spark ;
And few entrance, who take the minstrel's lute.
Prizes are rare, and many strive in vain ;
That many strive, shall critics stern complain,
And bid all bards, uncertified, be mute ?
Should I be so much blessed that one brief strain,
To souls devout or weary, solace lend ;
Or might be deemed, when thankful voices blend,
Fit vehicle for tuneful prayer or praise ;
An altar to "Contented Hope" I'll raise.
The simple daisy in the garden grows,
Beneath the stately pine, or fragrant rose.

NOTE.

These rhythmical meditations are not arranged according to their dates, which spread over a space of thirty years. Nor is there any classification of subjects, the apparent disorder being like Nature's order with " Cloud and Sunshine."

For the introduction of the piece entitled " Echo," the example is pleaded of so great a master as George Herbert.

A few of the pieces have already appeared in a small work entitled " Bolton Abbey Hymns ;" for some years out of print.

Many of them claim to be regarded only as devotional hymns. Without possessing the highest qualities of poetry, a hymn may be good when it is adapted to express or excite religious emotion. The Author will feel well rewarded, and his highest ambition satisfied, if one or two of the number should find their way into the psalmody of the Christian Church.

LONDON, *Nov.* 21, 1870.

CONTENTS.

Pilgrim Songs.

UNIVERSAL PRAISE.

" Praise ye the Lord ! Praise ye Him, sun and moon ;
Praise Him all ye stars of light ;
Fire and hail ; snow and vapours ;
Mountains and all hills ; beasts and all cattle ;
Bless the Lord, all His works ;
Bless the Lord, O my soul."

PRAISE the Lord, ye realms of Nature !
To your King glad homage pay ;
Sound His glory every creature,
Day proclaim it unto day ;
Sun, that speaks His fadeless splendour,
Moon, that mildly rules the night,
Circling planets, praises render,
Praise Him all ye stars of light !

B

Let the earth bend low before Him
　　Round its axle as it rolls ;
Isles and continents ! adore Him,
　　Blazing zone, and icy poles ;
Alpine peaks ! reflect His glory,
　　Burn, volcanoes, in His praise ;
Hill to valley shout the story,
　　Every land an altar raise !

Torrents foaming from the mountains,
　　Rivers winding through the plain,
Murmuring streams and bubbling fountains,
　　Hissing hail and fruitful rain ;
Praise Him ! rolling waves of ocean,
　　Crested billows, slumbering blue,
Blend ye waters in devotion,
　　Morning mists and diamond dew !

Let the months in long procession,
　　Each its proper tribute pay ;
Let the seasons in succession
　　On His altar offerings lay ;
Incense fit from each ascending,
　　Summer, led by tuneful Spring,
Gifted Autumn, grateful bending,
　　Winter wild, His praises sing !

Praise Him forests, dark, primeval,
   Spreading oak and pillared pine,
With the ancient world coeval ;
   Praise Him corn and clustered vine !
Roses praise Him ! fragrant bowers,
   Jessamine and lilies twine ;
All ye field and garden flowers,
   Him to praise your charms combine !

All your varied voices blending,
   Pealing thunder, whispering breeze,
Plaintive notes from flocks ascending,
   Murmur of the trembling trees ;
Raise the psalm of adoration
   Sounding sea, and tinkling rill !
Swell the chorus of Creation
   Tuneful grove, and echoing hill !

Bees amidst the blossoms humming,
   Linnets carolling the spring,
Cuckoo's shout of summer coming,
   Larks high soaring as ye sing ;
Nightingales with pensive rapture,
   Blackbird, thrush, and cooing dove,
Winged choristers of nature,
   Sing your Maker's psalm of love !

Ponderous whale and tiny minnow,
　Huge behemoth, gay gazelle,
All that dive beneath the billow,
　All that in the forest dwell ;
Insects in the sunshine dancing
　Merry in their mystic maze,
Flocks reposing, horses prancing,
　Join in nature's hymn of praise !

Praise Jehovah ! all creation ;
　Praise Him ! ye above the sky ;
Praise Him ! every tribe and nation ;
　Praise Him ! heaven, let earth reply ;
All ye seraph choirs adore Him !
　Saints triumphant robed in white !
Ransomed sinners ! bend before Him ;
　All in praise to God unite !

THE PRODIGAL.

"I will arise and go to my Father."

I'VE wandered far from home,
 I'm weary, sad and sore,
I weep—but yet I roam,
 Wounded—I wander more ;
From treacherous friends shall I seek comfort ? No !
I will arise and to my Father go.

I'll tell Him all my sin ;
 I'll show Him all my pain ;
Perhaps He'll let me in
 To the old home again ;
But all my guilt and misery I'll show ;
I will arise and to my Father go.

I've squandered all my store ;
 My every hope is quenched ;
Repulsed from every door,
 From all my moorings wrenched,
In my extremity of sin and woe
I will arise and to my Father go.

All worthless as I am,
    Poor, helpless, guilty, lost,
Through the atoning Lamb,
    And by the Holy Ghost,
Because my sins and sorrows overflow,
I will arise and to my Father go.

My Father's name is Love,
    His mercies aye endure ;
He calls me from above,
    His word of grace is sure ;
Leaving my sin and misery below,
I will arise and to my Father go.

MORNING VOICES.

"Cause me to hear Thy lovingkindness in the morning."

'TIS sweet, when morn begins to break,
By morn's own music to awake ;
Hearing the sigh of trembling trees
That whisper to the whispering breeze ;
The matin song of lark that soars
And at heaven's gate its rapture pours ;
The blackbird's mellow, tender note,
Response from many a tiny throat,
Till the full chorus of the grove
Bursts forth to praise the God of love :
But sweeter far at morn to hear
Thy lovingkindness, soft and clear.

When sleep's brief death departs with dawn,
And night's dark curtain is withdrawn,
How doth each faithful heart rejoice
To hear a friend's saluting voice ;
How blest in proof of love and life,
Greeting of husband and of wife ;
How musical to parents' ear
The treble tones of children dear ;
How sweet the mother's love expressed
To babe that nestles in her breast ;
But sweeter far at morn to hear
Thy lovingkindness, soft and clear.

Cause me, each morning, then to hear
Thy lovingkindness, Father dear !
Though oft forgetful, wayward, wild,
Assure me I am still Thy child ;
Tell me my sins are all forgiven ;
Bid me anew press on for heaven ;
O let Thy love my will control ;
Counsel, instruct, direct, console ;
Say—soon as dawn salutes the sight—
" I am Thy everlasting light ";
Thus every morning let me hear
Thy lovingkindness, soft and clear.

THE LAMB OF GOD.

"O Lamb of God that died to take away the sin of the world have mercy upon us! Grant us Thy peace."

O LAMB of God! that on the cross
Didst suffer to atone our loss,
Give ear unto a sinner's plea,
Have mercy, Lamb of God! on me.

There's room within Thy wounded side;
For all transgressors Thou hast died;
Pardon for all hast Thou unfurled
Whose blood was shed for all the world.

O Lamb of God! the gracious, mild,
The "holy, harmless, undefiled,"
Assist me to resemble Thee,
Have mercy, Lamb of God! on me.

O Lamb of God! grant me Thy peace,
From sin and sorrow send release,
And fit me for Thy home of rest
To be with Thee for ever blest:

There may I join the ransomed throng,
And swell the everlasting song—
" Worthy the Lamb who once was slain,
Worthy for evermore to reign!"

MOUNTAIN THOUGHTS.

AT PONTRESINA.

"Thy righteousness is like the great mountains."

Lord of the mountains! Thee I praise
Who didst the ancient hills upraise,
The furrowed cliffs that frown on high,
And granite peaks that pierce the sky.

The glaciers Thy dominion own,
The ice-domes are Thy glittering throne,
The avalanche thunder is Thy voice,
Thou bid'st the torrents wild rejoice.

Thine are the reservoirs of snow,
Whence never failing rivers flow
To fertilize, at Thy command,
In summer drought the level land.

Thou dost instruct the hardy pine
Between the rocks his roots to twine;
The forests dark Thy praises show,
Guarding the cultured fields below.

On pasture slopes of emerald green
Thy cattle feed, the firs between,
The chiming of whose tuneful bells
With worship fills the flowery dells.

Thou showest to the eagle where
He may his cloud-veiled nest prepare ;
Thou dost preserve, for chamois fleet,
The tender, snow-nurst moss, to eat.

The whistle of the marmot shrill
Thou hearest from its storm-rent hill,
And the cicala's sunny glee
Is watched, was caused, is loved by Thee.

Under the thick-ribbed glacier's shade
Thou hast enamelled carpets laid ;
And given to the gentian blue
Its smiling, heaven-reflected hue.

Thou, amidst precipices stern,
Wavest fair fronds of mountain fern ;
And, where the lightning leaves its scar,
Soft *edelweiss* reveals its star.

On rough moraine and dizzy steep,
Thy star-bespangled mosses creep :
These Alpine heights, if stern to view,
With Alpine flowers are lovely too.

So full of wondrous mystery,
Of beauty, strength, sublimity,
In these great mountains, Lord, I trace
Types of Thy righteousness and grace.

Stainless as yonder fields of snow,
Fairer than fairest flowers that grow,
More musical than mountain rills,
More lasting than the ancient hills.

But who *these* heights sublime may scale ?
Vision alike and reason fail !
Who can explore *these* gulfs profound ?
Who measure *these* vast mountains round ?

Though clouds their awful crests conceal,
To faith, their lower slopes reveal
The perfect wisdom, goodness, love,
Of Him who reigns supreme above.

God of the Mountains ! let me share
Thy righteousness and loving care !
Secure, by Thine almighty word,
Beneath the shadow of the Lord.

Then, when the hills at Thy command
Shall melt away, my soul shall stand ;
Because THY RIGHTEOUSNESS, my plea,
Abideth everlastingly.

QUESTION AND ANSWER.

WEARY and sad, dear Lord, I look to Thee !
      " Come near to me."
A question I would ask, my heart to cheer—
      " Speak ! do not fear."
When will my cheeks no more with grief be wet?
      " Patience ! not yet." .
When will the flesh and spirit cease their strife ?
      " At close of life."
Will not this long, fierce fight, till death be o'er?
      " No ! not before."
Shall I then ne'er attain to perfect rest ?
      " Yes ! with the blest."
I fear—I faint—my tears unceasing fall !
      " I know it all."
How trials so prolonged can I endure ?
      " My grace is sure."
How can I breast the dark and stormy tide ?
      " I'm at thy side."
Where may I lay my sword and armour by ?
      " In heaven on high."
When may I hope the victor's palm to wave ?
      " Beyond the grave."
When shall I bask in heaven beneath Thy smile ?
      " A little while—
" Then shalt thou rest and reign with me above,
      " Perfect in love."

THE PRIMROSE.

UNDER S. MARTIN'S HILL, SURREY.

I LOVE the early primrose
   That lightens up the lane,
So radiant in the sunshine,
   So cheerful after rain;
Good-bye to dreary winter
   How gladly doth it sing,
And tells of milder weather,
   And hopeful, happy Spring.

I wish that like the primrose
   My life was always bright,
And shone in darkest pathways
   With mild and constant light;
I wish that I reflected
   Each sun-ray from above,
I wish that 'neath the storm-cloud
   I always smiled with love.

I wish that in the valley
  As on the swelling hill,
Seen or unseen, with beauty
  I did my task fulfil;
In life's retired copses
  As in the garden gay,
Beside the forest foot-track
  As by the broad high-way.

I would be ever showing
  That winter's reign is o'er;
A happy pledge and promise
  Of joys for evermore;
I would be like the primrose,
  And sing in sun or shade,
Of spring that's everlasting,
  Of flowers that never fade.

THE SHADOW OF DEATH.

" Yea, though I walk through the valley of the shadow of death,
I will fear no evil, for Thou art with me."

Jesus! my Shepherd, strong to save,
Whose love Thyself for sinners gave,
In death's dark vale if Thou art near,
Weak though I be, no ill I fear.

Where thickets dense o'erhang the way,
With lions lurking for their prey ;
Where fiercer men and forms of hell,
In wait for souls, malignant dwell ;

Where not one straggling ray of light
Pierces the funeral pall of night ;
Where every moment of the gloom
Threatens some sadder, deadlier doom ;

The vale of anguish, dark and deep,
Where tears of blood are those we weep,
Where every footstep costs a groan,
And every pilgrim walks alone ;

E'en here the Shepherd's marks I feel,
And still Thyself Thou dost reveal ;
For Thou hast walked this very way, ·
And Thou art with me, Lord, to-day.

Thy voice of sympathy I hear,
My Brother, Thou art very near ;
Thy hand is gently laid on mine,
My faith, responsive, claspeth Thine.

Thy wounds, Thy bleeding side I see,
Thy rod, Thy staff, they comfort me ;
Thy human love, Thy cross, Thy crown,
Thy cruel shame, Thy great renown.

If Thou art near, my Shepherd, Guide,
No evil can my soul betide ;
The darkest valley leads to light,
Grief trains for glory ever bright.

And when I reach the stream called death,
I'll triumph in what Jesus saith—
" The Resurrection-Life am I,
He that believes shall never die."

SON OF DAVID! SON OF MARY! SON OF GOD!

SON of *David !* Jesu, Saviour !
  Unto me Thy mercy show ;
Heavy laden, Lord, I labour,
    Pity me and rest bestow ;
      Fount of healing !
  Let Thy streams within me flow.

Son of *Mary !* Tender Brother !
  Thou hast shared our human woes ;
Comfort, soothe me like a mother,
    Loving—shield me from my foes ;
      Man of sorrows !
  He has felt and therefore knows.

Son of *God !* Great King of glory !
  Lord Eternal ! Mighty Friend !
Lowly, joyful, I adore Thee,
    Might and mercy in Thee blend ;
      I will praise Thee !
  Hallelujah ! without end.

" MY TIMES ARE IN THY HAND."

" Commit thy way unto the Lord."
" Your heavenly Father knoweth."

My times are in Thy hand !
   I know not what a day
Or fleeting hour may bring to me,
But I am safe while trusting Thee,
   Should all things fade away.
     All weakness I
     On Him rely
Who fixed the earth, and spread the starry sky.

My times are in Thy hand !
   Pale poverty or wealth,
Corroding care or calm repose,
Spring's balmy breath or winter's snows,
   Sickness or buoyant health—
     Whate'er betide,
     If God provide,
'Tis for the best; I wish no lot beside.

My times are in Thy hand !
 Should friendship pure illume
And strew my path with fairest flowers,
Or should I spend life's dreary hours
 In solitude's dark gloom—
  Thou art a Friend,
  Till time shall end,
Unchangeable, in Thee all beauties blend.

My times are in Thy hand !
 Many or few my days,
I leave with Thee—this only pray,
That by Thy grace, I, every day
 Devoting to Thy praise,
  May ready be
  To welcome Thee,
Whene'er Thou com'st to set my spirit free.

My times are in Thy hand !
 Howe'er those times may end—
Sudden or slow my soul's release,
Midst anguish, frenzy, or in peace,
 I'm safe with Christ my Friend !
  If He is nigh,
  Howe'er I die,
'Twill be the dawn of heavenly ecstasy.

My times are in Thy hand!
   To Thee I can entrust
My slumbering clay, till Thy command
Bids all the dead before Thee stand,
   Awaking from the dust.
     Beholding Thee,
     What bliss 'twill be
With all Thy saints to spend eternity!

To spend eternity
   In Heaven's unclouded light!
From sorrow, sin, and frailty free,
Beholding and resembling Thee—
   O too transporting sight!
     Prospect too fair
     For flesh to bear—
Haste! haste! my Lord, and soon convey me
   there!

REFLECTING ALL THINGS FAIR.

AT ULLSWATER.

" Whatsoever things are lovely."

How deep, how pure, how tranquil is the lake !
Lowly beneath the great hills it doth lie,
Yet looketh day and night unto the sky,
Whose tints and glorious radiance it doth take.
The sun and stars a matchless mirror make
In its calm bosom, bending from on high ;
Yet none the less, earth's objects that are nigh
Are seen reflected there—the ferny brake,
The bending birch-tree and the steadfast pine,
The daisied meadows where the cattle feed,
The tiny pebbles on the beach that shine,
Each tuft of moss and every trembling reed.
So to my soul be such pure calmness given,
Reflecting all things fair in earth and heaven.

THE SUPPLIANT AND THE SAVIOUR.

"Lord! if Thou wilt, Thou canst make me clean."
"I will! be thou clean."

Lord, if Thou wilt, Thou canst restore
 My leprous, dying soul;
Stretch forth Thy gracious, healing hand,
 Thy touch can make me whole.

Lord, if Thou wilt, Thou canst efface
 Sin's dark and deadly stain;
Cleanse me from all defilement, Lord,
 Nor let one spot remain.

Lord, if Thou wilt, Thou canst renew
 My spirit by Thine own;
O give to me a heart of flesh,
 And break this heart of stone.

Lord, if Thou wilt, Thou canst conform
 My stubborn will to Thine;
Rule every thought, and may Thy light
 In all my actions shine.

Lord, if Thou wilt, Thou canst console
  In sorrow's darkest hour ;
O cheer me by Thy sympathy,
  Sustain me by Thy power.

Lord, if Thou wilt, the weakest saint
  Shall triumph over death ;
Joyful Thy praises may I sing,
  With my last parting breath.

Lord, if Thou wilt, Thou canst reclaim
  My body from the grave ;
The " Resurrection and the Life,"
  Mighty art Thou to save.

Thou canst! Thou wilt! almighty power
  Is linked with boundless love ;
By grace divine I'll serve Thee here,
  And dwell with Thee above!

HEAVENLY TREASURE.

"Lay up for yourselves treasures in Heaven, where
neither moth nor rust doth corrupt."

WHY should we lay up treasures here below,
  Where moth and rust corrupt? Why fix our heart
On joys from which so quickly we must part?
Why, on an ocean where such tempests blow,
  Embark so rich a freight? Why, midst the snow
Of so unkind a winter, plant a flower
So fragrant, yet so frail? Why build Hope's tower
  Where lightnings flash, and whelming torrents flow?
But if our highest energies are bent
  In God and Heaven a portion to secure,
Whate'er betide, our heritage is sure;
  When the destroying angels forth are sent,
  When melts away the starry firmament,
Our bliss unharmed, shall, e'en as God, endure.

FOLLOWING JESUS.

"If any man will come after me, let him deny himself, and take up his cross and follow me."

THY Holy Spirit, Lord, impart,
And stir with love my sluggish heart,
Then gladly from all sin I'll part,
   And rise to follow Thee.

I would obey Thy kind command
To march with Thee to Canaan's land—
But need Thy guiding, strengthening hand ;
   Help me to follow Thee !

My Teacher, Ruler, Pattern, Guide,
Ne'er let me wander from Thy side,
Nor from the narrow pathway slide,
   But closely follow Thee !

By meekness, patience, kindness, prayer—
By works of love and friendly care—
By holy conduct everywhere—
   Help me to follow Thee !

Whene'er the road is rough and steep,
Whene'er the floods roll strong and deep,
Although, distressed, I groan and weep,
       Still may I follow Thee!

When fears and foes beset the way,
When darkest clouds obscure the day,
And easier paths tempt me to stray,
       Help me to follow Thee!

At every hour, in every place,
Amidst all dangers, give me grace
With patient, plodding, onward pace,
       Closely to follow Thee.

Courageously, whoe'er my foes,
With cheerfulness, whate'er oppose,
Unto my journey's final close,
       Help me to follow Thee!

Then along Heaven's own pathway bright,
No more with foes and fears to fight,
By Victory crowned, and robed in white,
       I'll ever follow Thee!

---

* This hymn may be sung to a L. M. tune by repeating the word "follow" in the fourth line of each verse.

THY WAY IS BEST.

"Father, not my will, but Thine be done."

Thy way, O Lord! Thy way—not mine!
   Although, opprest,
For smoother, sunnier paths I pine,
   Thy way is best.

Though crossing thirsty deserts drear,
   Or mountain's crest;
Although I faint with toil and fear,
   Thy way is best.

Though not one open door befriend
   The passing guest;
Though night its darkest terror lend,
   Thy way is best.

So seeming wild without a plan,
   Now east, now west,
Joys born and slain, hopes blighted, *can*
   Thy way be best?

My soul by grief seems not to be
  More pure and blest ;
Alas ! I cannot, cannot see
  Thy way is best.

I cannot see—on every hand
  By anguish prest,
In vain I try to *understand*
  Thy way is best.

But I *believe*—Thy life and death,
  Thy love attest,
And every promise clearly saith—
  " Thy way is best."

I cannot see—but I believe ;
  If heavenly rest
Is reached by roads where most I grieve,
  Thy way is best.

THE BEST GIFT.

" My son, give me thy heart."
" There is none upon earth that I desire beside Thee."

WERE I, on God's high altar, to present
All I possess—if, as a sacrifice,
I offered up whate'er men chiefly prize—
Yea, if the splendours of the firmament,
The universe itself, if all were sent
As tribute to the Monarch of the skies—
Without my heart, such gifts He would despise:
Without such gifts, my heart would Him content.
So—I should still unsatisfied remain,
If riches, honour, fame, and friends were mine—
Of poverty my soul would still complain;
Beyond Thy gifts, for Thee, for Thee I pine:
Without Thyself, such gifts would all be vain;
Without such gifts, Thyself art endless gain.

THE PUBLICAN'S PRAYER.

" God be merciful unto me a sinner."

BENDING beneath a load of sin,
  Deserving for that sin to die,
Danger without, remorse within,
  To whom for succour can I fly ?
Father ! I lift my prayer to Thee—
O God ! be merciful to me.

No works of mine I dare to plead,
  Without excuse, condemned I stand ;
Save me in this my utmost need,
  Stretch forth to me Thy helping hand ;
Weak, guilty, lost—I cry to Thee—
O God ! be merciful to me.

Thy love is vast, Thy mercy free,
  I have no confidence beside ;
This, this alone is all my plea—
  For me the Saviour lived and died ;
In Jesu's name I cry to Thee—
O God ! be merciful to me.

LIVING BREAD AND HEAVENLY WINE.

HYMN FOR HOLY COMMUNION.

" My flesh is meat indeed, and my blood is drink indeed."

THOU, O Christ, art living Bread—
Let me from Thyself be fed!
Jesus, Thou art heavenly Wine—
Let me drink and know Thee mine!

Hungry—after Thee I long;
Feed me, and thus make me strong;
Thirsty—without Thee I'm sad,
Thou alone canst make me glad.

Lord! supply my urgent need,
For Thy Flesh is meat indeed:
Without Thee I faint, I sink,
For Thy Blood indeed is drink.

Jesus! 'tis for Thee I pine,
Be to me both Bread and Wine!
Nourish, cheer me with Thy love,
Till I feast with Thee above.

BOLTON ABBEY.

"All thy works shall praise thee, O Lord ; and thy saints shall bless thee."

ENTRANCED with varied loveliness, I gaze
On Bolton's hallowed fane.   Its hoary walls,
More eloquent, in ruin, than the halls
Of princely pomp, their solemn features raise
'Mid thick embowering elms.   Meek cattle graze
The peaceful pastures circling it around ;
Old Wharfe flows sparkling by with pensive sound,
And heathery hills look down through purple haze.
All lend their aid to prompt these humble lays ;
Some kind and soothing influence all have given—
The mouldering Abbey, and the moss-grown grave,
The breezy moorland, and the rock-nurst wave,
Cliff, meadow, forest—all direct to Heaven,
All blend their voices in one psalm of praise.

THE RUINED TEMPLE.

AT BOLTON ABBEY.

" Know ye not that ye are the temple of God ? "

LIKE some fair temple overthrown,
With broken arch and crumbling stone,
The soul, though reared by hands divine,
In ruin lies, a shattered shrine.

These walls now roofless, rent and bare,
Once echoed to the chanted prayer;
And joyful strains of holy song
Sublimely rolled these aisles along.

Kindled and nourished from above,
The altar-flame of Faith and Love
Within the heart was burning bright,
Diffusing round its tranquil light.

But sin that sacred flame has quenched,
And from its base that altar wrenched;
While reptiles foul and birds unclean,
In that once holy place are seen.

Yet, though polluted and defaced,
Its pristine form may yet be traced;
And, on its sculptured fragments, still
The Builder's name is legible.

Restore Thy ruined temple, Lord!
O speak the soul-transforming word;
Thy cleansing blood can expiate,
Thy Holy Spirit new-create.

Remove the deep and deadly stain
Of orgies dark, and rites profane;
Bid lust, pride, selfishness depart,
Drive every idol from my heart.

Let sacrilegious foot no more
Presume to tread that temple-floor;
Henceforth be no pollution found
To desecrate this holy ground.

Rebuild the altar, kindle there
The incense of habitual prayer;
And let the sacrifice of love
Accepted rise, through Christ above.

Let patient efforts to fulfil
Thy holy, wise, and gracious will,
A constant psalm of praise uplift,
More prized by Thee than pompous gift.

Let tower and pinnacle arise,
From earth up-soaring to the skies;
And every thought and purpose be
An aspiration unto Thee.

Thus, Lord! my ruined soul restore,
To be Thy home for evermore;
A glorious, consecrated shrine,
Eternally, completely Thine!

PRAYER TO THE HOLY SPIRIT.

"Take not thy Holy Spirit from me."

O THOU long suffering Spirit! still
    With this rebellious heart abide ;
Cease not to check my wayward will,
    Subdue my sins, destroy my pride.

Thy counsels oft I've madly spurned,
    Against Thy striving dared to fight,
Oft quenched the flame that in me burned,
    And to Thy grace done sore despite.

Yet leave me not, Thou heavenly Dove !
    Helpless, undone, to Thee I cry ;
Pardon my crimes against Thy love,
    Nor from the suppliant sinner fly.

My heart I now would open wide ;
    Great Sanctifier! enter in ;
Sprinkle the blood of Him who died,
    And take away the power of sin.

Thy living temple I would be ;
    O come and dwell within my breast ;
My Teacher, I'll be led by Thee,
    My Guide to heaven's eternal rest.

REST.

"There remaineth therefore a rest for the people of God."
"We which believe do enter into rest."

Rest! I cry to Thee for rest,
Calm, O calm this troubled breast!
Bid the anxious conflict cease,
Mid the tempest whisper "peace;"
Weary with the length of way,
Pining for the light of day,
Tempted, wounded, sin-distressed—
Lord! I pray, I pant for rest.

Bid my fluttering heart be still;
Make me cease from vain self-will;
Seeking Thee alone to please,
Loving all Thy love decrees,
Casting on Thee every care,
Sure that Thou my grief wilt share,
On Thy sympathising breast
Let me lean, and be at rest.

Soon to me, O Lord, be given
Rest with Thee, at home, in heaven!
Rest from sorrow, toil, and strife,
Rest from all the ills of life;
Every holy want supplied,
Every yearning satisfied,
Give the rest of God above,
Perfect rest in perfect love.

THE GOD OF ABRAM.

"The Lord said unto Abram, get thee out of thy country, unto a land that I will show thee; and I will bless thee, and thou shalt be a blessing."

"They which are of faith, the same are the children of Abram."

O God of Abram! let Thy word
By Abram's pilgrim-child be heard;
Let me obey the gracious call—
" Arise, go forth, forsaking all."

Forth from a world of sense and sin,
A heavenly heritage to win;
Leaving each idol vain behind,
My Father, in my God, to find.

Although untrod, unknown the way,
Though doubts and darkness shroud the day,
If Thou wilt lead me by the hand,
Promptly I'll follow Thy command.

Possessing Thee, all things are mine;
No foes can harm if I am Thine;
Call *me* Thy friend, and let me be
Blest, and a blessing made, by Thee.

While thus, a stranger here, I roam,
Be Thou my ever-present home;
And soon my weary footsteps guide
Where rest and holy peace abide.

Then, in the promised land above,
The changeless home of perfect love,
With all the Patriarch's ransomed race
I'll sing the glory of Thy grace.

All praise to Abram's God be given
By pilgrims here, and saints in heaven!
Let men with angels join to raise
The song of never-ending praise.

FAREWELL.

TO MY MOTHER, 1843.

FAREWELL! Farewell! a few more years
And we shall leave this vale of tears,
Where fondest friends are farthest parted,
And distance mocks the broken-hearted:
Ah! then together we shall dwell,
And never hear the word "Farewell."
For they who reach the realms above
Are never torn from those they love;
Distance and death no more can sever,
Theirs is blest intercourse for ever,
Friendship from all base mixture pure,
A union ever to endure.
Ah! who can all the rapture tell
Of homes where ne'er is heard—"Farewell."

REMONSTRANCE WITH MINISTERING SPIRITS.

ON THE DANGEROUS ILLNESS OF MY MOTHER, 1868.

FORBEAR! attendant angels, O forbear
To urge the saint to take her heavenly flight;
Still let her loving smile our eyes delight;
Still to our fond embrace such treasure spare,
And for such loss our troubled hearts prepare.
Yours are the glories of unclouded light;
Be not too eager, from our gloomy night
To snatch a star that shines with beams so rare.
More fit for your society we know,
But needed more by us who mourn below:
Your social wealth congenial prize will gain;
Our poverty, remediless will grow:
Once gone—our arms will stretch for her in vain;
Spare her! once yours, you ne'er will part again.

CHRISTMAS ANTHEM.

"Glory to God in the highest."

To God on high be glory!
  Peace and good-will to men!
Proclaim the wondrous story,
  Sound forth the song again—
Glory to God and Peace on Earth!
Rejoice! give thanks with holy mirth.

Creation's Lord! adore Him
  In human likeness made;
Men! Angels! bow before Him,
  In the rude manger laid;
Glory to God and Peace on Earth!
Rejoice! extol the wondrous birth.

How low our God is bending
  To take our misery!
How high is man ascending
  By this great mystery!
Glory! in Bethlehem's holy child
Sinners and God are reconciled.

Heaven's Lord, our nature wearing,
   Man's Brother has become,
That we, His glory sharing,
   May dwell in heaven, at home ;
Glory to God and Peace on Earth !
Eternal praise for Jesu's birth !

To God on high be glory !
   His love be magnified ;
Spread through the world the story ;
   Be Jesus glorified !
In praise of Christ, our new-born King,
Earth ! Heaven ! with Hallelujahs ring.

PRAYER ANSWERED IN DISAPPOINTMENT.

"One jewel more"—I asked, "to make me glad."
He took the one I had.
"Come quickly, Lord, and heal this wounded heart!"
Still more He made it smart.
"At length from trouble bid my soul repose."
Yet thicker came the blows.
"Grant me a life of active zeal," I said.
He laid me on sick bed.
I asked to soar in sunlight as the lark,
But groped on, dull and dark.
"At least give peace in victory over sin."
More loud grew battle's din.
"O let me rest with Thee in pastures green!"
Only steep crags are seen.
"Why with keen knife, dear Lord, dost prune me so?"
"That grace may quicker grow!"
"Why in my portion mix such bitter leaven?"
"To fit thee more for heaven."
"Lord, take Thy way with me, Thy way, not mine."
"My child! all things are thine—
"All in the end, though grievous, shall prove best,
And then—eternal rest."

DE PROFUNDIS.

"Out of the depths have I cried unto Thee, O Lord."

Out of the depths I cry to Thee, O Lord!
　The deepest depths of agony and woe;
My only hope is in Thy faithful word,
　Thy sympathy the only balm I know.

There is a gulf for ordered speech too deep;
　A furnace far too fierce but for a cry;
Sorrows in which 'twere luxury to weep;
　A darkness whence is only heard a sigh.

Give ear to plaints that from these depths arise,
　Nor leave me in the dark to grope alone;
On my affliction look with pitying eyes,
　And answer prayers condensed in sigh or groan.

THE PILGRIM'S SONG.

"The redeemed of the Lord shall come with singing unto Zion."

WHY, Pilgrims of Hope, weep ye thus on the way
To regions where sorrow ne'er darkens the day?
Why groan with the griefs that are fleeting and light,
While guiding to glory and endless delight?

Rejoice! fellow travellers, banish your sighs!
To the hills of Salvation, with hope lift your eyes;
And as ye press onward, exultingly sing
The love never changing of Jesus our King.

He waiteth to welcome His servants on high;
He now, as we journey, is constantly nigh;
Companion, Consoler, and Guide in the road
To mansions prepared for His people's abode.

Such comfort He gives as we journey along,
That the timid grow brave, and the weary ones strong;
With the music of promise He charmeth the ear,
Till faith beholds home and Jerusalem near.

Though the path of the pilgrim be stony and steep,
And the strongest may sometimes tremble and weep,
Yet praise we the *Road* as well as the *Rest*,
Already, as pilgrims, unspeakably blest.

Rocks, frowning afar, look kindlier near,
And smiling with flowers their fissures appear ;
On tracts the most barren bright mosses abound ;
With sorrows the saddest some comforts are found.

At times all advance may be seemingly closed,
By valleys contracting and cliffs interposed ;
But, as we go forward, the path opens out
To gardens of gladness, through defiles of doubt.

To the eye of the thoughtless, our journey may seem
The dreary delusion of children who dream ;
But they see not the beauties which pilgrims behold,
And they feel not our joys which can never be told.

How pure and refreshing the life-giving rills,
As with silvery songs they leap down from the hills !
What vigour and gladness their waters impart
To the traveller, wearied and fainting in heart !

Choice fruits overhang, inviting the taste
Of all who to God and Jerusalem haste ;
The Rose and the Lily their sweetness exhale,
And the music of Heaven is borne on the gale.

The lions may roar, but those lions are chained ;
Apollyon may rage, but his wrath is restrained ;
Through the dark vale of conflict we'll sing as we fight,
Till the Mountains Delectable burst on our sight.

What prospects unfold as upward we climb!
How varied, extensive, enchanting, sublime!
From the summits of Faith, looking back, we survey
The beauties adorning each part of the way.

Where the road was the roughest, and sternest the steep,
And cares most compelled us to fear and to weep—
Amid the dark defiles of grief and despair,
We see all the pathway well ordered and fair.

But when we look forward, what regions of light,
Bathed in tints of the rainbow, enravish the sight!
A Paradise teeming with beauties untold,
A city resplendent with jasper and gold.

Clear as crystal, the waters of life ever flow
From the throne of the Blessèd One, banishing woe;
And the banks of the stream are adorned by the tree
In whose shadow the nations are holy and free.

No pestilence poisons the health-breathing air;
No storms ever darken the scenery there;
The heat never scorches, the frost never chills,
But perpetual spring clothes the valleys and hills.

In this beautiful land ever fragrant and green,
The Celestial City all glorious is seen;
Its mansions and terraces mount up on high,
And its glittering turrets illumine the sky.

Each gate is a pearl surpassingly fair ;
Its walls are of sapphires and amethysts rare ;
Its pathways are gold, and its palaces blaze
With a lustre eclipsing the diamond's rays.

'Tis holiness renders the city so bright ;
True secret of splendour, pure source of delight !
Its gold and its jewels—its dignity, this—
The perfection of Love is the fulness of bliss.

But where is the tongue can the rapture unfold,
Of the numberless hosts who their Monarch behold ?
Reflecting His likeness, illumed by His smile,
Where sin, death, and sorrow no longer defile.

Bright squadrons of Angels, in countless array,
Meet with Prophets and Martyrs, long since passed away ;
The Saints of all ages, made perfect, are there ;
And the friends, gone before us, our welcome prepare.

By Faith even now is Jerusalem near ;
Its glories we see, its hosannahs we hear ;
And soon we shall rest in its palaces bright,
And drink at the fountain of endless delight.

Then rejoice ! fellow travellers ; banish your sighs !
To the hills of Salvation with hope lift your eyes !
And, as ye press onward, exultingly sing
The love never changing of Jesus our King.

E

THE BROTHER IN ADVERSITY.

"We have not an High Priest which cannot be touched with the feeling of our infirmities; let us therefore come boldly unto the throne of grace, that we may obtain mercy, and find grace to help in time of need."

WHEN crushed with care, and sunk in woe,
To whom for comfort can I go,
    But, dearest Lord, to Thee?
In all my griefs Thou hast a part,
And in Thy large and loving heart,
    There is a place for me.

O Jesu! Brother, Friend divine,
Within my lonely dungeon shine;
    Out of the depths I cry:
Let me not sink in dark despair,
Help me my heavy load to bear,
    Show me that Thou art nigh.

The furnace fierce I will not fear
If Thy consoling voice I hear;
    The flame will not consume;
The darkest night will turn to day,
Its fearful phantoms fade away,
    If Thou the gulf illume.

Amid the toil, the daily strife,
The bitter, bitter pains of life,
    Hold Thou my drooping head;
Be Thou my constant, tender friend,
Console, preserve me to the end,
    Stand near my dying bed.

Increase my faith, and give me grace
Thy love to trust, when least I trace
    Thy loving, faultless plan;
Make me by grief for glory meet—
Howe'er Thou wilt—in me complete
    The work Thy love began.

Come quickly Lord! and let me rest
From sin and sorrow, ever blest
    At home, in heaven, with Thee:
Then will I praise Thee as I ought
For these brief woes, o'er-ruled, that wrought
    Such blest Eternity.

THE CONTRAST.

"Set your affections on things above, not on things on the earth."

THE fairest flower that ever bloomed
  Must droop and die; the brightest day
  In evening gloom shall fade away
To death each new-born joy is doomed.

Wealth, faithless flatterer, soon takes wing;
  Or, where it lingers, cannot feed
  The immortal spirit's mighty need;
The golden sheath oft hides a sting.

Mirth is a bubble soon to burst;
  Friends most beloved may prove unkind;
  Death will the closest ties unbind;
Our best delights by sin are curst.

There is a flower which ne'er can fade;
  A priceless treasure none can steal;
  A balm which every wound can heal;
A hope on sure foundations laid.

There is a Friend—Life, Love, his name—
  Who cannot faint, or fail, or die ;
  But, strong to help, is always nigh ;
In grief and gladness still the same.

There is a home in Heaven above,
  Where kindred souls ne'er part again ;
  But, free from death, sin, care, and pain,
Dwell with this Friend in perfect love.

PRAYER FOR ENGLAND.

"God be merciful unto us and bless us, and cause His face to shine upon us."

God bless our dear old England!
　With cliffs so bold and white,
Round which the angry billows
　So vainly roar and fight:
God bless our sons and daughters,
　And make them pure and brave;
By righteousness, the nation,
　O righteous Father! save.

God bless our beauteous England!
　This cultured garden fair;
With orchard, meadow, corn-field,
　Lovely beyond compare;
Adorn her with the beauties
　Of holiness and grace,
These fruits and flowers reflecting,
　O Lord! Thy smiling face.

God bless our grand old England
  With proud historic name!
And may she yet outrival
  Her thousand years of fame;
But chiefly—make her steadfast
  In godliness and truth,
Wisdom of age uniting
  With all the zeal of youth.

God bless the wealth of England!
  Her industry and trade;
And ne'er by vile ambition
  May she her power degrade;
First in the roll of nations
  Let her by *justice* be;
Rich in good works, and pleasing,
  O God of Peace, to Thee.

God bless our home of freedom!
  Her oldest, dearest shrine;
Sacred by blood of martyrs
  Guarding the "Right Divine;"
Still may the flag of England
  O'er freemen only wave:
But chief, from sin's dominion
  Thy chartered people save.

God bless our land of churches !
    Where spire and tower are seen
Thick foresting the cities,
    And gladdening the green ;
Make all their pastors faithful,
    Bless every house of prayer ;
When Christians meet for worship
    Be with them everywhere.

God bless the Queen of England !
    Our noble and our great ;
Our senators and judges,
    And those who guide the State ;
Breathe over all their counsels
    Wisdom and patriot health,
Thy faith and fear directing
    Our regal Commonwealth.

God bless our English people !
    Brave, loyal, trusty folk ;
Free from all chain of bondage,
    Scorning each sinful yoke, .
May rich and poor together
    Labour and love as one,
A happy, royal priesthood,
    And so Thy will be done.

Old England! Heaven defend her!
  God bless our native land ;
Beside her in all danger
  Do Thou her Guardian stand.
God bless our dear old England !
  And may she ever be
Exalted 'midst the nations,
  By faith, O Lord, in Thee !

———

THE BEATITUDES.

"He whom thou blessest is blessed."

THOU who blessèd didst pronounce
Humble souls that pride renounce :
Poor in spirit let me be,
And Thy heavenly kingdom see.

Blest are they who mourn for sin,
They shall find true peace within :
Thus may I with grief o'erflow,
Thus true comfort may I know.

Blessèd are the meek in mind,
Lasting treasure they shall find :
Gentle Jesus! let me be
Meek and gentle, like to Thee.

Thou the hungry souls dost bless,
Souls that long for righteousness :
May I thirst and hunger so,
Thus Thy fulness may I know.

Blessèd are the merciful,
Prompt to pardon, pitiful :
Mercy, Lord, on me bestow,
Mercy may I ever show.

Blest are they whose hearts are pure,
They the sight of God secure :
May my heart be holy too,
Thus Thy glory may I view.

Blessèd are the sons of peace,
Bidding strife and anger cease :
Let me with Thy children be
Numbered, God of Peace, by Thee.

Blest are they who for their Lord
Suffer wrong in deed or word :
Zeal like theirs to me be given,
Prize like theirs be mine in heaven.

DAILY BREAD.

"Our Father which art in Heaven—give us this day our daily bread."

FATHER, throned in heaven above,
Might and Mercy, Light and Love !
Give to us, as Jesus said,
Day by day our daily bread.

Satisfy our daily need,
Soul and body daily feed,
Daily hear us when we pray,
Succour, save us, day by day.

Give us daily faith, to ask
Needful aid for daily task ;
Daily guidance in our way,
Daily warning lest we stray ;

Sympathy for daily grief,
Daily solace and relief,
Daily patience, meekness, zeal,
Others' griefs each day to feel ;

Daily help for daily cross,
Daily gain in seeming loss,
Daily strength for daily strife,
Daily grace till close of life.

THE SINNER'S FRIEND.

WRITTEN FOR MY FATHER, THE AUTHOR OF THE
TRACT "THE SINNER'S FRIEND."

"A Friend of Publicans and Sinners."

FRIEND of sinners! Lord of glory!
   Lowly, Mighty!—Brother, King!
Musing o'er Thy wondrous story,
   Grateful we Thy praises sing:
Friend to help us, comfort, save us,
   In whom power and pity blend—
Praise we must the grace which gave us
   Jesus Christ, the sinner's Friend.

Friend who never fails nor grieves us;
   Faithful, tender, constant, kind!—
Friend who at all times receives us,
   Friend who came the lost to find!—
Sorrow soothing, joys enhancing,
   Loving until life shall end,
Then conferring bliss entrancing,
   Still, in Heaven, the sinner's Friend!

O to love and serve Thee better!
From all evil set us free ;
Break, Lord, every sinful fetter ;
Be each thought conformed to Thee !
Looking for Thy bright appearing
May our spirits upward tend,
Till, no longer doubting, fearing,
We behold the sinner's Friend.

THE SINNER'S APPEAL TO THE SINNER'S FRIEND.

"O! spare me, that I may recover strength before I go hence and be no more."

FRIEND of sinners ! hear my cry,
Cast on me Thy pitying eye ;
Groaning 'neath a load of sin,
Foes without, and fears within—
Friend of sinners ! hear my cry,
Pardon, cleanse me, ere I die.

Friend indeed Thou art to me,
Yet how cold my love to Thee!
Shunning oft Thy kind embrace,
Slighting oft Thy Spirit's grace—
Friend of sinners! hear my cry,
Warm my heart before I die.

Send me succour from above,
Fill me with constraining love,
All my sinful passions quell,
By Thy Spirit in me dwell;
Friend of sinners! hear my cry,
Fully save me ere I die.

'Neath Thy shadow let me hide,
Happy ever at Thy side,
Faithful to the end of life,
Victor in the closing strife;
Sinners' Friend! O be Thou nigh;
Save, receive me, when I die!

ONWARD.

DURING A WALK IN A HURRICANE NEAR LLANDUDNO.

"Say unto the children of Israel that they go forward."

ONWARD! Christian pilgrim go,
Though the wild winds rudely blow;
Though the storm-clouds gather black,
Though the mist obscures the track,
Though the driving rain and hail
Make thy faith and courage quail,
Howsoe'er the tempests blow,
Onward, Christian pilgrim, go!

Now along the rocky shore
Angry waves tumultuous roar,
Flinging far their briny foam,
Dashing scorn on hopes of home;
Though across the narrow way
Drives the hissing, blinding spray—
Though the billows fiercely flow,
Onward, Christian pilgrim, go!

On! where rocks on rocks are piled,
Onward through the prickly wild,
Onward o'er the quivering bog,
Onward through the thickening fog,
Onward up the dizzy steep,
Onward where the torrents leap,
Though the danger seems to grow—
Onward, Christian pilgrim, go!

Home and safety yonder see!
There they wait to welcome thee :
Onward through the storm to calm!
On to win the victor's palm!
Brief the labour, long the rest ;
Scale the mansions of the blest!
Leaving tempest-clouds below,
Upward! Christian pilgrim, go!

MESSIAH'S REIGN.

AFTER HEARING THE HALLELUJAH CHORUS.

" King of kings, and Lord of lords ; and he shall reign for ever
and ever."

KING of kings, and Lord of lords !
What delight the sound affords !
Jesus shall for ever reign,
Final victory He shall gain.

Lord of lords, and King of kings !
Every mourner joyful sings ;
None shall of His rule complain
When the Saviour comes to reign.

King of kings, and Lord of lords !
Broken are oppression's cords ;
Sin is conquered, swell the strain !
Jesus doth for ever reign.

Lord of lords, and King of kings !
Order, riches, rest, He brings ;
Warfare, hatred, fear shall cease,
Vanquished by the Prince of Peace.

F

King of kings, and Lord of lords!
Earth and heaven repeat the words!
Truth and love will He restore,
He shall reign for evermore.

Lord of lords, and King of kings!
Loud and long the anthem rings;
Hallelujah! Shout again!
Jesus shall for ever reign.

———

THE NIAGARA OF SIN.

" Lord save us ; we perish."

SAVE, or I perish, Lord! the tide,
Smooth, treacherous, rapid, deadly, wide,
Hurries me headlong from Thy side;
      Save, or I perish Lord!

I slept on sin's delusive stream,
Gliding along as in a dream;
Waking—on hell's dark brink I seem;
      Save, or I perish Lord!

The howling fall I dare not brave,
Yet cannot stem the giant wave ;
Helpless—I cry to Thee to save ;
          Save, or I perish Lord !

Spirit of love ! I now implore
Thy aid, rejected, scorned before,
To snatch me from the rapid's roar—
          Save, or I perish Lord !

Jesus ! I faint, I sink, I die ;
Yet, sinking, fix my anguished eye
On Thee, and from the torrent cry—
          Save, or I perish Lord !

Thou canst ! Thou wilt ! Thy hand I see,
Long slighted, still held forth to me ;
I grasp that hand, I cling to Thee !
          Save, or I perish Lord !

THE SOWER.

THOUGHTS AT GRASSMERE CHURCH.

"He that goeth forth and weepeth, bearing precious seed, shall doubtless come again with rejoicing, bringing his sheaves with him."

WEEPING goes forth the sower on his way ;
Weeping—although he beareth precious seed ;
Weeping—because he knows his utter need ;
Weeping through many a dark and stormy day.
He weeps for goodly grain cast quite away ;
For barren foot-path, and delusive soil
Where rocks, scarce hidden, all his labour foil ;
For early bloom of hopes that will not stay ;
For thriving plants choked up by many a weed ;
Yet ceases not to sow, and watch, and pray.
The Saviour, as *He* sowed, did weep and bleed,
But now rejoices with the fruit alway :
So, like the Master, he who sows and grieves,
Shall doubtless come again with joyful sheaves.

"THE GOD OF OUR FATHERS."

" Our Fathers have told us what things Thou didst in their days,
and in the old time before them."

JEHOVAH, who to saints of old
Did oft His wondrous power unfold,
And help in utmost peril gave,
Is still as near and strong to save.

The ark amidst the furious flood
Securely rode, preserved by God ;
And, midst the wildest waves of care,
I cannot sink, if Thou be there.

Though, as a stranger, I may roam,
With Jacob's God I'm still at home ;
And, from each stony bed, doth rise
A radiant ladder to the skies.

In Egypt's bondage Thou art near,
The sighs of Israel Thou dost hear ;
And, while Thy plagues reach every foe,
Angels each blood-stained lintel know.

Thou, by a word, canst open wide
A pathway through the threatening tide;
And, whelmed beneath the surging sea,
Shall Pharaoh's chosen chariots be.

The barren rock shall yield supplies,
Pure fountains from its clefts shall rise,
Thy people shall be daily fed
In deserts wild, with heavenly bread.

When cast into the lion's den,
Or made the sport of fiercer men,
The lion's mouth Thy hand will close,
And guard me safe from all my foes.

When Satan's army gathers near,
When fails my fainting heart with fear,
Open Thy servant's eyes to see
The hosts of God, how strong they be!

He who till now has been our Friend
Will guide us safely to the end,
And land us on that peaceful shore
Where fears and foes afflict no more.

To God then let us joyful raise—
Our father's God—a song of praise;
And to our children tell His fame
Whose love is changelessly the same.

STAR-LIGHT MUSINGS.

AT PENENDEN HEATH, 1836.

"As the heaven is high above the earth, so great is His mercy
toward them that fear Him."

If light her pinions swift could lend
That to yon star I might ascend,
And then, through space my path pursue
Till Earth should vanish from my view :—

If, pausing on the Milky Way,
I might, with wondering gaze, survey
The countless orbs which throng the sky,
Beyond the ken of mortal eye :—

Thence mounting, could I wing my flight
Through unknown realms of starry light,
Upward, still upward, till I found
The vast creation's farthest bound :—

The loftiest point I thus might gain
Would still leave all my efforts vain,
The length, and breadth, and height to span
Of the Redeemer's love to man.

THE FADING LEAF.

" We all do fade as a leaf."

OUR life, how frail it is !
      Changeful and brief.
Spring, summer, fly—then we
      Fade as a leaf.

Why should a thought like this
      Minister grief,
If we our end fulfil,
      E'en as a leaf ?

Then, brightening at the close,
      Hoping relief
From sorrow, sin, and care,
      Fade as a leaf ?

Brief winter ; fadeless spring ;
      Blissful belief !
This is our *joy*, that we
      Fade as a leaf.

Of all our aims in life
      This then be chief—
Ripe, hopeful, bright, that we
      Fade as a leaf.

BLESSED ARE THE DEAD.

THOUGHTS IN KENSAL GREEN CEMETERY, AT THE
FUNERAL OF A FRIEND.

How blest are they who peaceful sleep !
   The long and sad life struggle o'er ;
Who neither toil, nor fight, nor weep ;
   Who fear, and faint, and fall no more.

From darkness, doubt, and care released ;
   From sin, and all temptation free ;
On fruits of Paradise they feast,
   And Jesus in His glory see.

Why should I cling to life on earth,
   With blighted hopes and yearnings vain ?
Where mourning swiftly follows mirth,
   And pleasures all are mixed with pain ?

O for the home of joy above !
   Its sacred calm, its holy rest ;
Where souls are linked in perfect love,
   And with their Lord are ever blest.

TEMPTATION.

"Watch and pray that ye enter not into temptation."

O THAT my soul were free from sin,
Completely purified within,
Completely rescued from the sway
Of him, whom death's dark realms obey!

Sin is my worst, my deadliest foe,
Sin caused the Saviour's blood to flow,
And sin would plunge me into hell,
In darkness and despair to dwell.

Shall I then welcome with a smile,
Satan advancing to beguile?
Or for one moment lingering stand,
When this destroyer's near at hand?

Shall I one moment stop to gaze
Upon his robe's deceitful blaze?
And trifle with the deadly dart
Which he is aiming at my heart?

Lord! give me grace that I may fly
Whene'er I see the tempter nigh;
Nor loiter on the dangerous ground
Where his enchanting snares abound.

Secure me safe within Thy fold,
My spirit to Thy likeness mould,
That sin may be my bitterest gall,
And Jesus be—my All in all.

CHRISTIAN VICTORY.

" To him that overcometh will I give to eat of the hidden manna,
and will give him a white stone, and in the stone a new name
written, which no man knoweth saving he that receiveth it."

SALVATION's Captain, mighty Lord !
Fulfil in me Thy gracious word,
Help me to wield the conqueror's sword,
Help me to overcome.

By Thee alone I hope to quell
The world, the flesh, the powers of hell ;
O let Thy Spirit in me dwell,
That I may overcome.

On Hidden Manna let me feed,
Thou only canst supply my need,
Thy blood, Thy flesh, are meat indeed ;
By Thee I'll overcome.

Give me to know my sins forgiven,
To see my foes all backward driven,
To glory in the hope of heaven,
   And thus to overcome.

Then, hailed by comrades gone before,
Convey me to that peaceful shore,
Where war's alarms are heard no more
   By those who overcome.

With warrior saints of high renown,
At victory's feast shall I sit down?
Shall I receive the conqueror's crown?
   Shall I thus overcome?

All honour, glory, praise to Thee,
To Thee alone shall rendered be,
Both now, and through eternity,
   By all who overcome!

THE LORD'S SECOND ADVENT.

" Behold I come quickly."
" Even so, come, Lord Jesus."

WHY, Lord, O why so long dost Thou delay
Thy promised coming ? why so long postpone
The glorious triumph by Thy Prophets shown,
And by the church expected ? Lord, we pray
That now, e'en now, may dawn Millennium's day.
Pity creation's long continued groan,
Answer the prayers that crowd around Thy throne,
Nor let Thy chariot wheels their advent stay.
O come to curb the serpent's cruel rage,
And sin, our deadly foe, in fetters bind ;
Wipe every tear away, all grief assuage,
Reveal Thy truth and love to all mankind ;
Let warfare, pride, oppression, envy cease ;
And fill distracted earth with heavenly peace.

"MY GRACE IS SUFFICIENT FOR THEE."

" For this thing I besought the Lord thrice, that it might depart from me. And He said unto me, My grace is sufficient for thee, for my strength is made perfect in weakness. Most gladly therefore will I rather glory in my infirmities that the power of Christ may rest upon me."

How oft in fear and woe I've cried—
   "Dear Lord deliver me ;"
But still thus only He replied—
   My grace sufficeth thee.

This thorn, which rankles in my heart,
   O Lord, with pity see,
And bid it speedily depart !
   My grace sufficeth thee.

Behold this bitter, bitter grief,
   This untold agony ;
O Jesus, swiftly send relief !
   My grace sufficeth thee.

How can I meet each boisterous wave
   On life's wild stormy sea ?
O calm the tempest ! succour ! save !
   My grace sufficeth thee.

The night is dark, the way is long,
    And friends and helpers flee!
The fight is fierce, the foe is strong!
    My grace sufficeth thee.

Enough, enough, what Jesus saith!
    I'll boast infirmity!
In conflict, sorrow, darkness, death,
    Thy grace sufficeth me.

"THAT I MAY WIN CHRIST."

A PARAPHRASE OF PHIL. III. 7—14.

" But what things were gain to me, those I counted loss for
Christ. Yea, doubtless, and I count all things but loss—that I may
win Christ."

WHEN my best actions, Lord, I see
    In Thy most searching holy light,
What was my gain is loss to me,
    And rendered hateful in my sight;
My own false worth I cast aside,
    The best is stained with self and sin;
My only plea is—" Christ has died;"
    My only aim is—Christ to win.

Jesus! my only Hiding Place,
    Jesus! who didst for sin atone,
I hope in Thy redeeming grace,
    I flee for help to Thee alone :
Cleanse me in Thy most precious blood,
    And make my nature pure within ;
Thus am I reconciled to God
    By faith, when Thee, O Christ, I win.

Yea, doubtless, all things else are loss
    That keep my soul, O Lord, from Thee ;
Joy beyond words is in Thy cross,
    'Tis heaven, Thy smiling face to see !
O let me know and love Thee more,
    Leaving the things that are behind,
And reaching forth to things before,
    Till Christ, the prize, I fully find.

With Thee, in fellowship of woe,
    Conformed to Thee, e'en unto death,
May I Thy resurrection know,
    And live for Thee in every breath ;
Thine image may I thus attain,
    To Thine own glory enter in ;
For all God has to give, I gain,
    And heaven is mine, when Christ I win.

SUNDAY MORNING.

SACRED Sabbath! Holy Rest!
With the smile of Heaven imprest;
Joyful Sunday!—radiant shine,
Gladden me with light divine.

Poor man's charter from above,
Sign to all that God is love;
God, who labour did ordain,
Bids the weary rest again.

Day when severed households meet,
Gathering round the Mercy-seat;
Day of calm retreat from care,
Day of cheerful praise and prayer.

Day of the Creator's rest,
When His finished work He blest;
Day on which the Saviour rose,
Victor over all His foes.

O may I, in God, my home,
Peaceful rest and never roam;
O that I with Christ may rise,
Till I join Him in the skies.

Fit me, Day of holy rest,
For the Sabbath of the blest ;
Be the Sun of all the seven,
Foretaste, harbinger of heaven !

SUNDAY EVENING.

Accept, O Lord, we humbly pray,
The service of Thy holy day ;
Our sacrifice of grateful praise,
The prayers, like incense, which we raise.

No merit may our service win,
Our sacred robes are stained by sin,
Discordant notes our praises mar,
In prayer our thoughts oft wander far.

Priest of the Church ! Thou, Thou alone,
Our faults and failings canst atone ;
Thou, Jesus, once for all didst bleed,
And still dost live to intercede.

O let our offerings perfumed be,
With fragrant incense, Lord, by Thee ;
And let our worship reach the skies,
Accepted through Thy sacrifice.

BEFORE SERMON.

Holy Spirit, now impart
Light and love to every heart;
Let the message we shall hear
Quicken, strengthen, guide and cheer.

Father! may we each fulfil
All Thy wise and loving will;
Be it everywhere obeyed,
Thus let Earth like Heaven be made.

Thou who on the cross didst bleed,
Now enthroned to intercede,
Hear our blended cry to Thee,
Hear our Heaven-indited plea.

Let Thy kingdom come, O Lord;
Mighty be Thy conquering word;
Hasten on the golden age;
Claim Thy purchased heritage!

AFTER SERMON.

PRAISE to Thee, Most High, be given,
For the gospel sent from heaven ;
For the message we have heard,
For Thy pure, life-giving word.

Praise for pardon, full and free,
Loud proclaimed from Calvary ;
Praise for Jesus—Saviour, Friend ;
Praise for love that ne'er shall end.

Holy Ghost, Thy grace impart ;
Seal the truth on every heart ;
May we all on Christ rely,
For Him live, and in Him die.

Praise the Father ! Praise the Son !
Praise the Spirit ! Three in One !
By us all may praise be given,
Now on earth ; for aye in heaven.

PLEA FOR THE WANDERING.

" Considering thyself lest thou also be tempted."

PITY the wandering—O! the bitter strife,
The shame, the fear, the anguish of their life.

Pray for the wandering—Jesus prays for *thee*;
If He should weary grow, where would'st *thou* be?

Excuse the wandering, far as hope can go;
Perhaps their foes were more than thou canst know.

Plead for the wandering—Law on Love will smile,
If pity prompt, not licence thee beguile.

Console the wandering—theirs is grief indeed,
And, oft forsaken, be their friend in need.

Assist the wandering—thou may'st need a hand,
For thou may'st fall, who firmly now dost stand.

Be patient with the wandering—God with thee
Is patient, not from sin art *thou* quite free.

Seek out the wandering—love them, succour lend,
And thus resemble Christ, the wanderer's Friend.

Reclaim the wandering—thou hast been reclaimed,
And Jesus sought thee, found thee, cheered, not
    blamed.

O save the wandering—bliss indeed 'twill be,
With souls thus won, to spend eternity.

PRAYER FOR THE PRAYERLESS.

WE pray for those who do not pray,
Who waste, O Lord, salvation's day :
For those we love who love not Thee—
Our grief, their danger, pitying see !

Those for whom many tears are shed,
And blessings breathed upon their head ;
The children of Thy people, save
From godless life, and hopeless grave.

Hear fathers, mothers, as they pray
For sons, for daughters, far away ;
Brother for brother, friend for friend—
Hear all our prayers that upward blend.

We pray for those who long have heard,
But still neglect, Thy gracious word ;
Soften the hearts obdurate made
By calls unheeded, vows delayed.

Release the drunkard from his chain,
Save those beguiled by pleasures vain,
Set free the slaves of lust, and bring
Back to their home the wandering.

The hopeless cheer ; guide those who doubt ;
Restore the lost ; cast no one out :
For all that are far off we pray,
Since we were once far off as they.

———

HOLY SPIRIT, SUCCOUR ME !

"The Spirit helpeth our infirmities."

HOLY Spirit ! succour me,
Compassed with infirmity ;
I am foolish, feeble, blind—
Be my Helper—faithful, kind !

Help me to repent of sin,
Help me to be pure within,
Every lust may I forsake,
Every evil habit break.

Help me patiently to bear
Sorrow, pain, and anxious care ;
Help me to be strong in faith,
Trusting all my Saviour saith.

Ever may I Him obey,
Never from His foot-marks stray,
My affections fixed above,
May I serve because I love.

SORROW AND SUCCOUR.

I SINK!
Lord! from the brink
Of sin and dark despair,
O hear my earnest prayer;
And lift me up to purity,
And bid me trust, and hope, and rest in Thee.

I fear!
O Lord, be near
To shield me from my foes;
Ward off their cruel blows,
And give me grace to stand and fight,
And make me more than conqueror by Thy might.

I weep!
The floods are deep;
Stretch forth Thy hand and save;
Bear me above the wave;
I'll sing for joy amid my tears,
If in my grief my heavenly Friend appears.

I die!
Jesus be nigh!
Then, victor in the strife,
Winning eternal life,
Glad hallelujahs I will sing,
And soar to live and reign with Christ my King.

"DEATH IS SWALLOWED UP IN VICTORY."

THOUGHTS IN HIGHGATE CEMETERY.

ARE death's dark emblems suited for the grave
Of those who dwell in heaven's unclouded light?
For souls arrayed in robes of dazzling white
Shall blackest palls, and plumes funereal wave?
Shall lilies drooping with untimely blight,
Torches reversed, whose flame is quenched in night,
And columns shattered, our compassion crave
For those whom Christ, by death, did fully save—
Who now, made perfect, serve, and in His sight
Drink of the fountain of supreme delight?
Rear high the shaft! "NEW LIFE" thereon engrave!
Turn up the torch! it never burnt so bright;
A richer hue and scent the lily gives;
Not till the Christian dies he fully lives!

TO BE WITH CHRIST.

"Having a desire to depart and to be with Christ, which is far better."

To be with Christ! O glorious hope!
What other joy with this may cope?
  The brightest star
That gleams in this world's night is dim,
Earth's bliss is mean—to be with Him
  Is better far.

Better than riches, power or fame,
Better than wear the proudest name,
  Is Christ to see;
To feel the assurance of His love,
And thus to share the joys above,—
  With Christ to be!

To be with Christ, is better *now*,
Though pain and anguish cloud the brow,
  Than worlds to own;
Better with Him to toil and fight,
To fast through longest, darkest night,
  Than feast alone.

O how much better still to be
With Christ—from sin and sorrow free—
　　In heaven our home!
To see His face, His glory share,
And from His blissful presence there,
　　No more to roam.

———

CHILDREN'S APPEAL TO THE CHILDREN'S FRIEND.

"Suffer the little children to come unto me."

Jesus! Friend of children! hear us,
　　As we lift our cry to Thee;
May we know that Thou art near us,
　　And Thy smile of pity see;
　　　　Friend of children!
Suffer us to come to Thee.

We are very young and tender,
    Help our helpless infancy;
Take the tiny gifts we render,
    Our great Saviour ever be;
        Friend of infants!
    Suffer us to come to Thee.

Let not friend nor foe prevent us,
    As to Thy kind arms we flee;
Give us, Lord, the blessing sent us,
    Hear, O hear, our humble plea;
        Friend of children!
    Suffer us to come to Thee.

Babes and sucklings, Jesu! fold us
    In Thy bosom tenderly;
We believe, for Thou hast told us,
    That Thy love is full and free;
        Friend of infants!
    Suffer us to come to Thee.

Old and young, now swell the chorus,
    Shout aloud in harmony!
Hallelujah! Lord, reign o'er us,
    Now and through eternity;
        Friend of all men!
    We will ever worship Thee.

THE CHILD'S HOSANNAH.

"Out of the mouth of babes and sucklings Thou hast
perfected praise."

PRAISE to Jesus! blend your voices;
   Christ, the great Redeemer, praise!
Ransomed earth with heaven rejoices;
   Bring your loudest, sweetest lays.
       Children's voices,
       Infants' voices,
May their glad hosannahs raise.

Let us sing the wondrous story
   Of the child's almighty Friend;
How He left the realms of glory,
   And to die did condescend.
       Children's voices,
       Infants' voices,
Sing the love that ne'er shall end.

Babes and sucklings! sound His praises;
   He for us a babe became;
Us in His kind arms He raises,
   Now, as when on earth, the same.
       Little voices,
       Infants' voices,
Sing the Son of David's name.

From His glory He beholds us—
" Suffer them to come to me "—
Still in His kind bosom folds us ;
Our best Friend will ever be.
Babes and sucklings,
Little children,
Hope in heaven that Friend to see.

Worthy is the Friend who sought us—
Wandering, weary, helpless, lost ;
Worthy is the Lamb who bought us—
His own blood the countless cost.
Children's voices,
Infants' voices,
Blend with the angelic host.

Praise to Jesus ! swell your voices !
Old and young the Saviour praise:
Ransomed earth with heaven rejoices ;
Bring your loudest, sweetest lays.
Infants' voices,
Children's voices,
All combined, hosannah raise.

ECHO.

SAY, Echo! where is joy with no sad leaven?
Heaven!
Heavy the griefs that work out such delight.
Light!
Too great the cost, the flesh to crucify.
Fie!
Satan hath Destiny for strong ally.
A lie!
They say sin's sweet and safe—and I believe it.
Leave it!
I cannot, will not leave the soil I grew in.
Ruin!
Honour and ease I'll not exchange for shame.
For shame!
After such toil must I lose all again?
A gain!
I think I'm good enough, in word, in deed.
Indeed?
You doubt it, Echo! wisdom much you need.
You need!
Say! must I first all doctrine rightly know?
No!
How keep myself from falling, Satan's prey?
Pray!
And will God hear me if to Him I cry?
Aye!
And will He help if I to Him complain?
Plain!
Shall I succeed if I by prayer endeavour?
Ever!
I'll work, I'll fight, my weapons shall not rust!
Trust!

RETURN UNTO THY REST, O MY SOUL.

WEARY and sad, with guilt opprest,
Return my soul unto thy rest;
And lay thy load on Christ alone,
Who for thee suffered to atone.

Wounded, and faint, and sick, and sore,
Seek help at Mercy's open door;
Jesus alone can make thee whole,
Return unto thy rest, my soul!

Perplexed with doubts and reasonings vain,
In childhood's faith come back again;
A lamb upon the Shepherd's breast,
Return, my soul, unto thy rest.

Fretted with vanity and pride,
Come, kneel apart at Jesu's side;
There, lowliness and meekness learn,
And thus unto thy rest return.

Betrayed in quest of worldly joy,
Whose brightest gold is base alloy,
Return, my soul, unto thy rest ;
In Jesu's love be fully blest.

Weary with weeping, crushed with woes,
Thou hast a Friend who sees and knows,
And bids thee all thy sorrows roll
On Him, thy true rest, O my soul.

For He has felt the pains we feel,
And every wound will surely heal ;
Whate'er His love ordains is best ;
Return, my soul, unto thy rest !

Speed on brief night ! dawn endless day !
Grief, conflict, sin—soon pass away !
Then, with thy Lord, in glory blest,
Return, my soul, unto thy rest !

IN A STRAIT BETWIXT TWO.

" I am in a strait betwixt two, having a desire to depart and to be with Christ, which is far better: nevertheless, to abide in the flesh is more needful for you."

I LOVE my home below,
 The pleasant scenes of earth,
The nooks I so well know,
 Dear country of my birth;
I love her fields and flowers,
 Broad streams and tiny rills;
I love her woodland bowers,
 Green dales and breezy hills.
But there's a home on high,
 More beautiful and bright;
No tempests cloud the sky,
 The day ne'er sets in night;
There, is no sound of strife,
 No tears bedew the ground;
Beneath the tree of life
 Unfading flowers abound.

How strong the cords that bind
   Kindred and bosom friend!
Blest sympathy of mind,
   When thought and feeling blend;
More precious far than gold,
   The friendship of the heart;
I cannot loose my hold,
   I cannot bear to part.
But heaven has other friends
   Who beckon me to go;
Their circle still *extends*,
   While *lessens* this below:
There, is no bleeding heart,
   Graves are unknown above;
They meet and never part
   In that pure home of love.

Thy presence, Lord! how sweet,
   How blissful, though unseen,
When with Thy saints we meet,
   Or, lonely, on Thee lean;
The whispers of Thy voice
   Are music to my ear;
In darkness I rejoice
   When Thou, my Lord, art near.

But these delights how brief!
　　Hindered by sin and care;
How seldom such relief
　　Our wearied spirits share;
The glory will not stay,
　　The night grows dark again,
The vision fades away,
　　We stretch our arms in vain.

O to behold Thee shine,
　　For ever, where Thou art!
To know Thee always mine,
　　And never more depart;
To gain the prize long sought,
　　Thy perfect image share,
To love Thee as I ought—
　　'Tis better to be *there!*
Far better to depart
　　And with my Lord to be!
But—if by toil and smart
　　I still may honour Thee;
If to the least of Thine
　　I may some service do,
I would my wish resign,
　　In happy "*strait 'twixt two.*"

THE COMFORTER, THE HOLY GHOST.

SPIRIT of God! whose power alone
Can new-create this heart of stone;
O listen to my earnest cry,
Nor leave me in my sins to die.

Spirit of Light! dispel the cloud,
That darkly doth my soul enshroud;
Spirit of Holiness! expel
All evil thoughts that in me dwell.

Spirit of Prayer! instruct me how
Before the throne of God to bow;
And, pleading Jesu's precious name,
His purchased blessings humbly claim.

Consoling Spirit! peace impart,
When care and grief distract my heart;
Assure me of a Saviour's love,
And cheer with hope of joys above.

Of Heaven the Earnest and the Seal,
Let me Thy constant influence feel;
And, of the future world's high bliss,
Give me some foretaste, e'en in this.

Thus, Holy Ghost! Thy work complete,
Thus make my soul for glory meet ;
Then, to the Father, Son, and Thee,
I'll render praise eternally.

———

GRACE BEFORE MEAT.

God be praised for table spread !
  Bounteous Source of every good,
Give to all their daily bread,
  Bless our fellowship and food.
OR,
Father ! by whose care we live,
With our food Thy blessing give ;
Help the needy, and impart
Love and joy to every heart.

GRACE AFTER MEAT.

For food and friends let thanks be given !
  Lord ! may our lives be hymns of praise ;
Thus may we meet at length in heaven,
  And feast with Thee through endless days.

THE CHURCH, THE BRIDE OF CHRIST.

"I will show thee the bride, the Lamb's wife. And he showed me that great city, the holy Jerusalem, descending out of heaven from God, having the glory of God."

O BRIDE of Christ! how beautiful art thou!
Of myrrh and cassia thy garments smell,
From ivory palaces where thou dost dwell.
A queenly crown adorns thy radiant brow ;
Thy retinue king's daughters vie to swell ;
With cheerful gifts to thee all nations bow ;
No tongue thy peerless charms can fitly tell.
But whence thy glory?   Given thee from above :
Not the mock jewels which the worldly prize,
Thy charms are goodness, meekness, truth and love.
Alas! that we should hide, by rags of earth,
The beauty that is thine by heavenly birth.
Bridegroom Divine! strip off each vile disguise,
That her true charms may win all hearts and eyes.

"THOU ART MY HIDING PLACE."

From curse of law, and fear of hell,
Where can a sinner safely dwell?
With terror wild, dismayed, undone,
O where, for refuge, can I run?

Almighty Ruler! unto Thee
For safety and for peace I flee:
Though I deserve Thine angry frown,
On me, with pardoning love, look down.

In Thee alone, so long defied,
In Thee I may securely hide;
From Thee I fled in guilty fear;
To Thee, in faith, I now draw near.

Thy sovereign, free, unbounded grace,
This is my only hiding place;
O let me never from Thee roam;
Be Thou my soul's eternal home.

WHY PRAY? AN ARGUMENT.

" In everything by prayer and supplication, with thanksgiving,
let your requests be made known unto God."

Why pray ?   As if each small affair
Of little man, might claim the care
Of Him who reigns in boundless state !
   If not—is He so great ?

But *can* the God who guides the sphere
Of universal nature, hear
As if I only were in sight ?
   Is He not infinite ?

But how shall He who ruleth all,
Who guards the great, observe the small ?
How *can* He tend each single soul ?
   If not—how rule the whole ?

But if my prayer He *can* thus hear,
Say—*will* He deign to bend His ear ?
Give me some proof more strong than creeds !
   Thy heart within thee pleads.

But is there proof in mere desire
For that to which my hopes aspire ?
May I thus trust my nature weak ?
   'Tis God in thee doth speak.

From God that heavenly instinct came :
He wrote on thee His holy name ;
That conscious need, those yearnings strong,
        He gave, and will not wrong.

PRAYER FOR AN INFANT.

TO MY LITTLE NEPHEW W. N. H.

BABY Newman, tiny Willie!
New blown, tender, laughing lily!
May no frost of winter blight thee,
No fierce sun of summer smite thee,
No rude hand of man pollute thee,
No wild tempest ere uproot thee.
He who was Himself a child,
" Holy, harmless, undefiled,"
Bless thy childhood, bless thy youth,
Crown thy manhood with the truth ;
Make thee holy, keep thee pure,
Help thee to the end endure ;
Give thee life, by goodness long,
Soothing grief, resisting wrong ;
Loving sire and grandsire's God,
Treading the old path they trod ;
Then, with all who baby love,
May'st thou dwell in Heaven above.

A LITTLE CHILD'S MORNING HYMN.

Day again is dawning,
  Darkness flies away;
Now from sleep awaking,
  Let me rise and pray.
Jesu! tender Shepherd,
  Watching while I slept,
Bless the little lambkin,
  Thou hast safely kept.

Help me, Lord, to praise Thee,
  For my cosy bed;
For my clothes and playthings,
  For my daily bread;
For my darling mother,
  For my father dear;
For the friends who love me,
  Far away and near.

Robin blithe is chirping,
   Glad the night is o'er;
Larks the light are greeting,
   Singing as they soar:
I'm Thy little birdie;
   May I ever sing,
Goodness making music,
   Unto Christ my King.

Daisies now are turning,
   Bright eyes to the sun;
And the light is shining,
   On them every one:
I'm thy little flower,
   Jesus! shine on me—
Turning, all my lifetime,
   Grateful eyes to Thee.

God the Father loves me,
   Jesus died for me;
And the Holy Spirit,
   Guides and comforts me.
Glory to the Father!
   Glory to the Son!
Glory to the Spirit!
   Blessèd Three in One.   AMEN.

THE CHURCH, THE GARDEN OF THE LORD.

AT LYDNEY PARK CONFERENCE.

"Grace be with all them that love our Lord Jesus Christ in
sincerity."

THE garden of the Lord spreads far and wide ;
But not in one huge bed, unvaried, grow
The trees which He has planted ; fruits and flowers,
The lily, rose, and jasmine—fragrant bowers,
In differing borders the same beauty show.
Such varying forms true oneness cannot hide ;
They beautify the garden, not divide.
We hedge and fence our favorite bed—but lo !
Beyond the barrier, to reprove our pride,
Are flowers as sweet and fair ; the heaven-taught bees,
Seeking the honey, scorn the fence ; the breeze,
Incense from all alike to God doth blow ;
On all the beds He pours His showers divine,
On all the garden makes His sun to shine.

"I WILL LAY ME DOWN IN PEACE AND SLEEP."

When night has quenched the sun's last ray,
  And boding shadows round me creep,
Secure, as in the blaze of day,
  I'll lay me down in peace and sleep.

When round me varied trials crowd,
  And my crushed heart in sorrow steep,
With God, beneath the darkest cloud,
  I'll lay me down in peace and sleep.

When rudest waves my bark assail,
  And round me yawns the stormiest deep,
Amid the roaring of the gale,
  I'll lay me down in peace and sleep.

Compassed by fiercest powers of hell,
  From harm Thou canst Thy children keep ;
Thou makest me in safety dwell ;
  I'll lay me down in peace and sleep.

And when my day of life is o'er,
  And friends endeared around me weep,
To wake with Thee on Canaan's shore,
  I'll lay me down in peace and sleep.

SERVE THE LORD WITH GLADNESS.

" Serve the Lord with gladness, come before His
presence with singing."

SERVE the Lord with gladness!
  Joyful tribute bring ;
Banish fear and sadness,
  Grateful praises sing.
Serve the Lord with gladness!
  Cheerful anthems raise;
All His wide dominion,
  Swell the psalm of praise !
    CHORUS.
    Serve the Lord with gladness !
    Joyful tribute bring ;
    Banish fear and sadness,
    Grateful praises sing.

Serve the Lord with gladness!
  Banish servile fear;
Trust your tender Father,
  We to Him are dear.
All our sins He pardons,
  All our frailty knows ;
Helps in all our conflicts,
  Soothes in all our woes.
    CHORUS.
    Serve the Lord with gladness, &c.

Serve the Lord with gladness!
  Serve, and thus be free ;
Unreserved surrender,
  Noblest liberty !
All His laws are blessings,
  Each command a boon ;
Sorrows work our welfare,
  Bringing glory soon.
      CHORUS.
    Serve the Lord with gladness, &c.

Serve the Lord with gladness!
  Leave the world behind ;
Sin and self renouncing,
  Serve with heart and mind :
Serving Him is heaven ;
  Life is in His love ;
Endless joys are given,
  Deathless homes above.
      CHORUS.
    Serve the Lord with gladness !
     Joyful tribute bring ;
    Banish fear and sadness,
     Grateful praises sing.

NOW!

"Behold now is the accepted time,
now is the day of salvation."

Can the farmer hope to gain
Precious crops of golden grain,
If he idly, day by day,
All the seed-time dreams away?
Rouse thee soul! redeem the past'
Harvest time is coming fast;
Through the fallow drive the plough—
Wouldst thou reap? be sowing NOW!

Canst thou safe in port arrive
If thy ship at random drive?
Spread thy sail, fair blows the breeze,
Now the favouring moment seize!
Wouldst thou hear the word—"well done?"
Be the labour now begun!
Wouldst thou bind around thy brow
Victory's wreath? take helmet NOW!

Time's swift tide is surging o'er
Life's contracting, sinking shore;
Be thy guilt however great,
Now be saved—'Tis not too late.
Yet beware! lest mercy's day
Soon will all have passed away:
If thou wouldst escape, allow
Not a moment's slumber NOW!

Though repulsed so oft before,
Jesus knocketh at the door,
Bearing gifts untold, divine,
Treasures which may now be thine;
Wilt thou rudely from thee send
Such a generous, patient Friend?
Still He waiteth—wilt not thou
Welcome, worship, serve Him NOW?

GROWTH FROM WITHIN.

THE sports that childhood's hours beguiled,
Could only satisfy the child ;
   The man they fail to please :
And he who heavenly comfort knows,
The toys of worldliness outgrows ;
   Their vanity he sees.

The lamps which gaily deck the night,
Grow pale, and vanish from the sight,
   Quenched by the orb of day :
And earthly pomps no longer shine,
When Christ, the soul's true Sun divine,
   Our darkness drives away.

As wintry trees which cannot shed
Their withered foliage, dry and dead,
   Until new buds appear ;
So, we shall ne'er cast off our sin,
But by new life at work within—
   Faith, Hope, and Love sincere.

The barren branch is barren still,
Though on each twig, with rarest skill,
　We tie on flowers and fruit:
And all in vain we toil and strive,
By outward works to seem alive,
　If rotten at the root.

Giver of Life! my heart renew,
That I may render service true,
　The outgrowth of the soul:
Let love to Thee false love expel,
And folly find no room to dwell,
　Where Christ pervades the whole.

A HOLIDAY PSALM.

PRAISE God! Creator, Saviour, Lord,
Upholding all things by His word;
Now let our hearts unite to raise,
With all His works, a song of praise.

Praise God! who spread the azure sky,
And reared the swelling hills on high;
Who taught the rivers where to flow,
And the great sea his bounds to know.

Praise God! whose pencil paints each flower,
Whose breath perfumes each fragrant bower,
Who decks the lily and the rose,
And nurtures every plant that grows.

Praise God! whose varied voice is heard
In murmuring rill, and song of bird;
In ocean's roar, and summer breeze,
And soothing music of the trees.

Praise God! whose gifts the fields adorn,
Who clothes the vales with golden corn,
Who feeds the flocks on flowery hills,
And all His works with bounty fills.

Praise God! for health, and friends, and home;
For joy and safety when we roam;
For eyes to see, and hearts to feel
The love our Father's works reveal.

Praise God! who makes this world so fair,
That oft we fain would linger there;
Praise God! who hath salvation given,
And brighter homes, through Christ, in Heaven.

Praise God! from whom all blessings flow;
Praise Him! all creatures here below;
Praise Him above! ye heavenly host;
Praise Father, Son, and Holy Ghost!

·OUR ROYAL WIDOW BLESS.

ANTHEM ON OCCASION OF THE DEATH OF THE PRINCE
CONSORT; AND DURING THE EXCITEMENT CAUSED BY
THE AFFAIR OF "THE TRENT," ENDANGERING OUR
PEACEFUL RELATIONS WITH THE UNITED STATES.

GOD save our gracious Queen !
Long live our noble Queen !
God save the Queen !
Lord ! heal her bleeding heart,
Assuage its grievous smart,
Thy heavenly peace impart,
God save the Queen !

Our Royal Widow bless !
God guard the Fatherless !
God save the Queen !
Shield them with loving care,
Their mighty grief we share,
Lord hear the people's prayer,
God save the Queen !

O Lord our God, arise !
Bless England's enemies !
　　　On Thee we call :
Let sorrow whisper—Peace ;
Bid Wrong and Anger cease ;
Let Truth and Love increase ;
　　　Make Evil fall !

In this our Nation's need,
With Thee we humbly plead !
　　　God bless our Queen !
Her life-woe sanctify,
Her loss untold supply,
THYSELF be ever nigh
　　　To save our Queen !

THE MOUNTAIN PATHS OF LIFE.

THOUGHTS WHILE CROSSING THE ALPS IN WINTER.

" Hold Thou me up and I shall be safe."

ALONG the mountain paths of life,
Over the pass with perils rife,
Christ is my hope midst toil and strife,
    And none beside.

When wildest winds of winter blow,
Driving the thickly falling snow ;
When gather gloomiest clouds of woe,
    With me abide.

When the deep drift conceals the way
And death attends each step astray,
O Jesu! hear me when I pray ;
    Be Thou my Guide.

When treacherous ice o'erlays the ground,
When hangs the path o'er gulfs profound,
Cast Thy protecting arms around;
    Let me not slide.

The threatening avalanche hold back,
Through the thick fog reveal the track,
Smile Thou amid the tempest's wrack,
    Keep at my side !

When fails my heart with grief and fear,
Be Thou my Refuge, very near ;
Let me Thy voice of welcome hear,
    And in Thee hide.

When bitter blasts the blood congeal,
When lost is e'en the power to feel,
In death's dark hour Thy love reveal ;
    Thou—Thou hast died !

The mountain crossed, in restful bowers
Smiling with fruit and fadeless flowers,
I'll praise, with never wearying powers,
    My Saviour guide.

THE CRY OF THE TEMPEST-TOST.

COMPOSED DURING A HURRICANE ON THE ADRIATIC.

"Driven up and down in Adria."

Tost with many a wave,
While the loud winds rave,
  Sick and weary with the motion
  Of the never resting ocean,
Help from Heaven I crave.

Now I mount on high,
Now in gulfs I lie;
  Vainly toiling, fainting, weeping,
  Hostile tempests o'er me sweeping,
Hear my suppliant cry!

Lord I look to Thee!
Thou didst make the sea;
  Thou didst calm the stormy billow,
  Waking from Thy weary pillow;
Calm the storm for me!

When the gale is high,
On the wave draw nigh ;
   Meet my gaze of grateful wonder,
   Let me hear amidst the thunder—
" Fear not, it is I."

Through the storm and dark,
Be my soul's true Ark ;
   Though the hissing waves break o'er me,
   Thou hast felt their force before me ;
Steer my quivering bark !

When the light grows less,
In my utmost stress,
   When the clouds of death shall darken,
   In the gloom of midnight hearken !
Help, and save, and bless.

Guide me swiftly o'er !
Bring me safe to shore !
   Storms all past, to me be given
   Thee to see, and serve in Heaven,
Praising evermore.

THE UNKNOWN GOD.

THOUGHTS ON MAR'S HILL, GOOD FRIDAY, 1870.

"I found an altar with this inscription, To the Unknown
God. Whom therefore ye ignorantly worship, him declare I
unto you."

THE *unknown God!* unknown, though near !
   So near, that every one in Thee
Doth live and move, at length appear,
   Nor let us still in darkness be.
Open the eyes that sin hath closed,
   Unstop the ear so heedless grown,
Renew the will to heaven opposed,
   And be no more a *God unknown.*

Help me to see, in Jesu's face,
   The glory of the Father shine ;
Make me to feel Thy saving grace,
   And humbly, surely, call Thee mine.
Within the veil Thy name impart,
   Unto Thy children breathed alone ;
Thy covenant write upon my heart,
   And God, as Love, henceforth be known.

More than the outward ear has heard,
  More than mere intellect can see,
The hidden treasures of Thy word
  Show, by the Holy Ghost, to me.
Bear inward witness to the soul
  That Thou art mine, and I Thine own;
The length, the breadth, the wondrous whole—
  Reveal to me Thy love unknown.

Bestow the joy unspeakable,
  The peace of God, surpassing thought;
Converse with heaven which none can tell,
  Oneness with Thee by Jesus wrought:
And soon may I Thy glory see,
  And bend before the sapphire throne:
Thus now, and in eternity,
  Be not to me a *God unknown.*

ATHENS AND S. PAUL.

THOUGHTS AT ATHENS.

" And they took him, and brought him unto Areopagus."

ATHENS! How grandly beautiful art thou!
Thy dignity, in death, retaining long,
In spite of centuries of cruel wrong ;
In spite of earthquake, lightning, war, e'en now
Riseth sublime thy queenly, peerless brow.
What names and memories to thee belong—
Poets, and statesmen ; fields, renowned in song,
Where Athens guarded Greece from tyrant's thrall :
Demosthenes ; eventful Marathon ;
Plato and Socrates ; great Salamis!
Still awes the soul thy pillared Parthenon ;
Thy glittering, temple-crowned Acropolis :
But of thy glories this surpasseth all—
Rough, naked Areopagus, and—PAUL !

"SOMEWHAT AGAINST THEE."

AFTER VISITING EPHESUS.

"Unto the angel of the church of Ephesus write . . . I have somewhat against thee."

LORD! hast Thou somewhat against *me*?
   Thou, who dost know my works and heart?
In vain I shroud my thoughts from Thee,
   The Sun, from whom all shades depart.

Somewhat against me? Jesus—Thou
   Who for my sins didst bleed and die?
And who art interceding now,
   Preparing blissful seats on high?

Pardon, and peace, and life I owe,
   And all my joys, and hopes to Thee;
Thy love a ceaseless fount doth flow,
   And hast Thou somewhat against *me*?

Christ is no censor cold, and stern,
   Eager our faults alone to spy;
He loves each virtue to discern,
   Faith's smallest gift secures His eye.

I need not, with excusing breath,
  Plead all His works of grace in me ;
" I know thy patience"—Jesus saith—
  " Yet have I somewhat against thee."

Help me, O Lord, myself to know,
  And mourn my fault with grief sincere :
Let tears that mean amendment flow,
  Let fruits of penitence appear.

Show what Thou hast against me, Lord ;
  Let me renounce whate'er it be
That merits Thy reproving word ;
  O let me hate what grieveth Thee!

THE CRY OF THE CAPTIVE.

AT CAIRO.

"The children of Israel sighed by reason of the bondage, and their cry came up unto God, and God heard their groaning."

GOD of the captive, who didst hear
Thine Israel's groan, and mark each tear,
And pitying count each cruel stroke,
When crushed beneath proud Pharaoh's yoke;

O hear the captive sinner's cry!
Burdened by guilt and fear we sigh;
In Egypt's tombs we darkly grope,
Toiling without reward or hope.

The iron chain we cannot break;
The tale of bricks we cannot make;
Daily the tyrant's tasks increase;
Vainly we struggle for release.

We hate, but yet endure the chain;
We break, but bear the yoke again;
We loathe the bondage stern and vile,
With which our souls we still defile.

O God of Israel! strong to save,
Helpless—Thy promised grace we crave;
Our hopes are fixed alone on Thee;
Draw near! and set the captives free.

DAVID AND GOLIATH.

A METRICAL PARAPHRASE; FOR TWO LITTLE NEPHEWS.
AFTER VISITING THE SUPPOSED BATTLE-FIELD.

PHILISTIA's mighty hosts were spread
   Along the mountain side;
And down the dale their chariots swept,
   And horsemen fierce did ride.

Gath sent her giant, great and grim;
   Of Anak's sons was he:
His spear was like a weaver's beam,
   Or as a tall pine tree.

Each morn he stalked the middle ground,
   Which trembled as he trod;
And, brandishing his spear, defied
   Israel, and Israel's God.

High up the opposing mountain slope
   Were ranged the ranks of Saul,
Guarding the road to Israel's homes,
   Against oppression's thrall.

But not a man in all their host
   The challenge durst accept;
Back from the giant's frown they shrank,
   While fear upon them crept.

One day a ruddy shepherd lad
  Came to the camp, to bring
Provisions to his brothers three,
  Who fought for Ark and King.

His father's errand filled the heart
  Of David with delight;
For much he longed to see the camp,
  And learn how heroes fight.

He heard Goliath's blasphemy,
  And marked his haughty frown;
And wondered none rushed forth to cast
  The Pagan boaster down.

If no one else would do the deed,
  A simple shepherd boy,
Armed with the might of Israel's God,
  Would Israel's foe destroy.

"The Lord," said he, "by whom I slew
  "The lion and the bear,
"Will help me, for His people's sake,
  "This boaster's blows to dare."

So down he went unto the brook,
  And chose a pebble stone;
And with his sling went forth to fight,
  Trusting in God alone.

The giant scorned the simple lad
  Who thus appeared in view,
And cursed him by his idol gods ;
  And still his anger grew.

Young David said—" Thou meetest me
  " With spear and shield and sword ;
" But I come forth to vanquish thee,
  " Trusting in Israel's Lord."

One look of faith to heaven he sent,
  Then slung his pebble round,
Which sank into the giant's head,
  And stretched him on the ground.

In random rout the heathen host
  Despairing, turned to flee ;
While Israel swift pursued with shouts
  Of joy, and victory.

O God of Israel ! strong to save,
  Hear Thou my suppliant cry,
When Satan and the hosts of hell
  The church of God defy.

I am but as a little child,
  Yet will not yield to fear,
If Israel's God will be to me,
  Breastplate, and shield, and spear.

The simplest means ordained by Thee,
   The pebble and the sling,
Wielded by faith, shall win the day,
   And giants prostrate fling.

Then unto Israel's God will I
   Joyful hosannahs raise;
And, through a long eternity,
   Will Christ the Conqueror praise.

O ye who wave the victor's palm,
   And ye who still do fight;
From palace-home, from battle-field,
   Your voices all unite!

Loud hallelujah, glory, power,
   To David's Lord be given!
'Tis He who sends the victory;
   Praise Him—both Earth and Heaven!

BETHLEHEM. A CHRISTMAS CAROL.

"Unto you is born this day in the city of David a Saviour, which is Christ the Lord." "Glory to God in the highest, and on earth peace."

NOT in halls of regal splendour,
　　Not to princes of the earth,
Did the herald angels render,
　　Tidings of their Monarch's birth ;
Not to statesman, priest, or sage,
They proclaimed the golden age,
'Twas the poor man's heritage—
　　For on shepherds lowly,
　　Burst the anthem holy—
In excelsis gloria,
Et in terra pax !

Not by worldly wealth or wisdom,
　　Not by power of law, or sword ;
But by service, to win freedom ;
　　And by sorrow, bliss afford :
Born to poverty and pain,
Born to die and thus to reign,
Rescuing man from Satan's chain—
　　Jesus now rules o'er us,
　　Swell the joyful chorus—
In excelsis gloria,
Et in terra pax !

Glory be to God in heaven,
   Peace on earth, good will to men !
In the highest, praise be given !
   Angels ! strike your harps again.
Justice has on mercy smiled,
God and men are reconciled,
Through Emmanuel, new-born child.
   Blend we then our voices !
   Earth with heaven rejoices—
In excelsis gloria,
Et in terra pax !

Bid the new-born Monarch welcome,
   Pay Him homage every heart !
Hallelujah ! let His kingdom,
   Swiftly spread in every part.
War and bloodshed then shall cease,
Selfishness its slaves release,
Love shall reign, and white-robed peace ;
   Then, from earth as heaven,
   Praise shall aye be given—
In excelsis gloria,
Et in terra pax !

THE BEST WINE LAST.

CANA OF GALILEE.

" Thou hast kept the good wine until now. This beginning
of miracles did Jesus in Cana of Galilee."

WHEN Jesus, at the wedding feast,
   Displayed His power divine ;
And, moved with human kindness, turned
   The water into wine ;
The master of the banquet thus
   His wondering joy exprest—
" Unlike all others, Thou hast kept
   Unto the last Thy best."

Unlike the world and sin—they *first*
   Their gaudiest gifts display ;
But soon the falsehood we detect,
   The brightness fades away ;
The meteor's glare is quenched in night,
   Down every hope is cast ;
But Thou, O Lord, dost ever keep,
   Thy best wine to the last.

The battle brief and glorious, ends
 In victory, sure and long ;
Grief does but stretch and tune the chords
 For heaven's eternal song;
Bright sunshine follows fertile showers,
 Sweet toil wins sweeter rest ;
Kind snow doth nourish fadeless flowers,
 God's last are always best.

Better, when seeming worst, Thy wine
 Than the world's best can be ;
The bitterest cup brings health and joy,
 When mingled, Lord, by Thee.
If saved by grace from sin and guilt,
 All care on Thee I cast ;
Pour out for me, Lord, as Thou wilt,
 But keep the best till last.

THE NIGHT WAS VERY VERY DARK.

THE LAKE OF GALILEE.

"He saw them toiling in rowing, for the wind was contrary
unto them."

THE night was very very dark,
   Loud did the tempest roar;
And big waves tossed the little bark
   Back from the friendly shore.

The boatmen rowed with all their might,
   They tried and tried again
Throughout that dark and dangerous night;
   Yet all their toil was vain.

But Jesus saw each angry wave,
   Watchful and kind is He;
And came, His trembling friends to save,
   Walking along the sea.

Still more they feared the unknown Form
   Crossing the billows high,
Till Jesus spake amidst the storm—
   " Be not afraid, 'tis I!"

O how did then their hearts rejoice,
    And with fresh wonder fill,
When the wild storm obeyed his voice,
    And winds and waves were still.

Thus when my soul is tempest-tost,
    Dear Jesus, come to me !
Let me not mid the waves be lost,
    But calm the troubled sea.

Enter my boat, sit by my side,
    Hold Thou my feeble hand !
Then safely, swiftly, through the tide,
    I'll reach the heavenly land.

IT IS I.

THE LAKE OF GALILEE.

"Jesus spake unto them, saying, Be of good cheer; It is I; be not afraid."

SAVIOUR! when wildest storms of care,
Would sink my soul in deep despair,
O let me hear Thy voice declare—
        " 'Tis I!—be not afraid !"

Say to my troubled soul—" Tis I !
" *Love* rides upon the gloomy sky—
" Not wrath, nor chance, nor destiny—
        " ' Tis I!—be not afraid !"

When wave on wave assails my bark,
When frightful forms howl through the dark,
Let me Thy loving accents mark—
        " ' Tis I!—be not afraid !"

" 'Tis I—thy steadfast, loving Friend,
" Round thee my arms of might extend,
" My words with the loud thunder blend,
        " ' Tis I!—be not afraid !"

" For thee I once was tempest-driven ;
" With hostile winds I too have striven ;
" Grief, keener far, my soul hath riven—
        " ' Tis I!—be not afraid !"

" Human like thee—I sympathize ;
" Divine—I rule the stormy skies ;
" Lift up thine heart, and dry thine eyes—
             " 'Tis I !—be not afraid !"

" I come to bid the waves be still,
" Thine anxious soul with peace to fill,
" And turn to good each seeming ill—
             " 'Tis I !—be not afraid !"

" The gale shall speed thee on the way,
" The lightning lend a helpful ray,
" The dark more quickly bring the day—
             " 'Tis I !—be not afraid !"

" Soon shall the storm be changed to calm,
" The oar of toil to conqueror's palm,
" The prayer of fear to rapture's psalm—
             " 'Tis I !—be not afraid !"

" In heaven shall roll no stormy sea ;
" Thy peace shall there unbroken be ;
" At home eternally with Me,
             " Thou ne'er shalt be afraid !"

THE GOOD SAMARITAN.

BETWEEN JERUSALEM AND JERICHO.

" But a certain Samaritan, as he journeyed, came where
he was ; and when he saw him, he had compassion on him."

From Jerusalem the peaceful,
By a path too often trod,
Down to Jericho I journeyed,
City of the curse of God.

Leaving Salem far behind me,
As I blindly onward prest,
Robbers strong and stern assailed me,
Who that dark ravine infest.

Of my treasure they bereft me,
Wounded me in heart and head ;
Naked, wounded, faint, they left me,
Surely thinking I was dead.

Sad indeed was my condition,
Stripped of every hope I lay ;
Guilty, yet without contrition ;
Trembling, yet I could not pray.

Moses passed me, but he only
 Proved how helpless was my case;
Aaron in his robes swept by me,
 Saw—but slackened not his pace.

Prophets, Priests, Apostles, Martyrs,
 Noble and triumphant throng,
Sympathized—but could not save me,
 Kindly looked—but passed along.

Saints and Angels, all united,
 Could not save—they all passed by;
But, with love and joy, they pointed
 Unto One who now drew nigh.

Lo! He comes, despised, rejected,
 Angels' Lord, yet spurned by man;
Sinners proud will have no dealings
 With this scorned 'Samaritan.'

He beheld me, pitied, loved me,
 Promptly to my succour ran,
And revealed Himself unto me—
 CHRIST, THE GOOD SAMARITAN.

Great Physician! wounds the deepest
 Thou hast skill and power to heal;
O'er my bleeding soul Thou weepest,
 True compassion Thou dost feel.

Wine pour on me, probing, cleansing,
  Though my wounds may smart with pain ;
Then, with healing oil anoint me ;
  Pardoned, I'll rejoice again.

Wrap me in the spotless raiment
  Of Thy righteousness complete ;
Though I ne'er can render payment,
  Clothe me, Lord, from head to feet.

From the mire of sin uplift me,
  All my woes and weakness bear ;
In Thyself, sole Refuge, hide me ;
  All I need is treasured there.

Though, unseen, Thou often seemest
  Like a traveller passed away,
Ever near me, Thou suppliest
  All my wants from day to day.

Let me taste Thy love unceasing ;
  Feed me, clothe me, guard, console ;
Though my debt be still increasing,
  Jesus has endorsed the whole.

When in glory Thou returnest,
  Show that all demands are paid ;
Answer to the claims of Justice,
  That my guilt on Thee is laid.

L

From the inn, to Thine own Palace,
　　Then remove me, heavenly Friend!
Having pitied once and loved me,
　　Thou wilt love me to the end.

Then I'll sing with all the ransomed,
　　Sovereign Love's completed plan;
And adore, with ceaseless rapture,
　　CHRIST, THE GOOD SAMARITAN!

PART II.

May the love of such a Saviour
　　Prompt me to the love of man;
May I copy the behaviour
　　Of this Good Samaritan!

May I be to all a neighbour,
　　Feel I *ought*, because I *can;*
And for other's welfare labour
　　Like this Good Samaritan!

THE HOME AND FRIENDS OF JESUS.

THOUGHTS AT BETHANY.

" He went out of the city into Bethany ; and he lodged there."

THE crest of Olivet concealed
   A favoured little town from view,
Where bloomed bright flowers of the field,
   And olive groves and palm trees grew ;
There Lazarus, Mary, Martha made
A home where Jesus often stayed :
O that the Lord would dwell with me,
As with His friends at Bethany !

The door they loved to open wide,
   His first approach with joy to greet,
Their choicest offerings to provide,
   Or sit and listen at His feet :
Like them I fain would always feel,
And learn by love, and serve with zeal ;
Thus, help me, Lord, to welcome Thee,
As did Thy friends at Bethany !

The Son of God, adored above,
    Yearning, as man, for friendship here,
Did Mary, Martha, Lazarus love;
    And still His human friends are dear:
Their smile is pleasing in His sight,
Their heart's response yields Him delight;
O may I thus give joy to Thee,
As did Thy friends at Bethany.

With more than brother's tender heart
    He sympathized in all their grief;
Of every sorrow bore a part,
    In every trouble brought relief;
With them He viewed where Lazarus slept,
And, with the weepers, Jesus wept:
Dear Friend of mourners! comfort me,
As Thou didst them at Bethany.

Make me to know Thy wondrous name,
    "THE RESURRECTION AND THE LIFE;"
In change, decay and death the same;
    My Victor-Champion in the strife:
To me Thy gracious word apply—
"He that believes shall never die;"
And let Thy love be life to me,
As to Thy friends at Bethany.

THE GARDEN OF GETHSEMANE.

"O my Father, if it be possible, let this cup pass from
me: nevertheless, not as I will, but as Thou wilt."

FATHER, let this cup pass from me,
    Filled to the brim with gall;
To taste alone is misery,
    How can I drink it all?

I hold it with a trembling hand,
    Amazement chills my heart;
O let this cup, at Thy command,
    This bitter cup depart!

Fiercer than torments flesh can know,
    Are those the mind assail;
The bloody sweat revealed a woe
    Keener than scourge and nail.

If it be possible, O Lord,
    Let this cup pass from me;
Hear Thine own agonizing word
    From dark Gethsemane!

Yet Father, not my will, but Thine,
    Thy will alone be done;
And make Thy loving purpose *mine*,
    Through Jesus Christ, Thy Son!

THE TRIUMPH OF THE CRUCIFIED.

GOLGOTHA.

"God forbid that I should glory save in the cross of our Lord
Jesus Christ."

Redeemed from death, with joy we'll sing
The triumphs of our suffering King;
His wounded hands—His bleeding side—
The wondrous cross on which He died.

Those wounds are fountains, whence do flow
Rivers of balm for human woe;
That blood can make the vilest pure,
That blood alone can cleanse and cure.

Those hands, extended on the tree,
Hold out a pardon full and free;
And, stained with sacrificial blood,
Obtain and publish peace with God.

The spear's deep gash that gapes so wide,
Invites the fugitive to hide
In God incarnate—there alone
Sure refuge from our fear is known.

The crown of thorns proclaims a King
Victorious by suffering ;
Henceforth shall grief to Christians be
Arrayed with regal dignity.

The cross becomes a conqueror's car,
Returning from successful war,
Where Christ, all red with battle-stains,
Drags Sin and Death in captive chains.

That dying groan, that last loud cry,
Are the glad shout of Victory ;
The bruisèd heel grinds Satan's head,
And life is won by Jesus dead.

Then let us, glad and grateful, sing
The triumphs of our suffering King ;
Count all things else as empty dross,
And glory only in the Cross.

"THIS SAME JESUS."

"This same Jesus, which is taken up from you into heaven, shall
so come in like manner as ye have seen Him go into heaven."

Jesus, our risen, glorious Lord,
　Ascended to Thy throne,
By saints and seraphim adored,
　Monarch supreme! alone!
We laud Thy greatness, we adore,
　But most we bless Thy *Name;*
For Thou art what Thou wast before,
　Our Jesus—still the same:

The same who to the leper said,
　And touched him—*Be thou clean;*
The same whose kind hand gently led
　The blind man, poor and mean;
The same who fed the fainting crowd,
　Who healed the halt and lame,
Whose word dispelled the stormy cloud,
　Our Jesus—still the same.

The lonely widow's bleeding heart
  His heart of pity knew;
He touched the bier, bade death depart,
  And her son lived anew:
And still, to share our human grief,
  He hath a human claim;
And still His pity sends relief,
  For He is still the same,

Who came with gentleness to call
  The lost and wandering home;
And toiled in kindly quest of all
  From truth and heaven that roam;
Whose feet the woman bathed with tears,
  Who shielded her from shame,
Who spake her pardon, calmed her fears—
  JESUS is still the same:

The same who did the children call
  To nestle in His breast;
And bade the heavy laden, all,
  Come unto Him for rest:
His title was the Sinner's Friend!
  To save the lost He came;
His love will never never end,
  JESUS is still the same:

The same who sorrowed at the grave
 Where His friend Lazarus slept;
And godlike consolation gave,
 While human tears He wept:
And still He joins the funeral train,
 And weeps with those that weep;
And whispers—*" He shall rise again "*—
 For death is only sleep.

He shared our human misery,
 Hunger He knew, and thirst;
He groaned in dark Gethsemane,
 His heart with sorrow burst ;
Our inward conflicts, yearnings, woes,
 The frailty of our frame,
Our Brother felt, and still He knows,
 And still remains the same :

The same who bowed His head to die,
 And stained the bitter cross
With streams of human agony
 To compensate our loss ;
Who for His murderers did pray,
 Nor uttered word of blame ;
Jesus! our Advocate this day,
 Unchangeably the same.

In human form heaven worships Thee !
   Still, God our nature shows ;
Our Brother not ashamed to be,
   Mindful of human woes ;
As man He mounted to the sky,
   E'en as a man He came ;
And soon again shall every eye
   Behold Him, still the same.

Thy sympathy, unchanging Friend !
   Is strength, and joy, and rest ;
Thy love, till life's long toil shall end,
   Makes e'en our sorrows blest ;
And when at last shall melt away
   Creation's mighty frame,
We'll praise, through heaven's eternal day,
   Our JESUS—still the same.

"THAT GOODLY MOUNTAIN."

SUNDAY THOUGHTS IN THE LEBANON.

" I pray Thee let me go over and see the good land that is beyond Jordan, that goodly Mountain, and Lebanon."

WEARY with wandering o'er the sand,
Pining to reach the promised land,
My longed-for home at length so near,
This prayer, my Guide, my Father, hear.

Soon let me cross the stream and see
The land beyond that beckons me,
So fair above comparison,
" That goodly mount and Lebanon."

I long to tread its fragrant fields,
To taste the ambrosial fruit it yields,
To rest beneath the tree of life,
From guilt and grief, from toil and strife.

I long to meet, to embrace once more,
Dear fellow travellers gone before ;
With them rehearse our pilgrim ways,
And join again in Jesu's praise.

O that the goal were fully won,
That goodly, glorious Lebanon !
Whose beauties never shall decay,
Whose treasures none can take away.

No lion fierce, nor ravening bear,
No wily serpent harbours there :
No murderous thief in ambush lies,
The incautious traveller to surprise.

No fierce sirocco's burning breath
Shall bring decay, disease, and death ;
No summer-droughts the fountains dry,—
The streams flow everlastingly.

No locust cloud shall dim the air,
Leaving the hopeful branches bare ;
No wintry frosts shall nip the bloom,
No blazing heat the crops consume.

Those stately cedars ne'er shall feel
The stroke of wasteful woodman's steel ;
Those peaceful pastures ne'er shall dread
The thunder of the foeman's tread.

Those heavenly heights I long to climb,
To reach those glittering peaks sublime,
Still up those shining slopes to press,
The mountain of God's holiness.

There " Carmel's excellency" blends
With all the charms that " Sharon" lends :
O for that never-setting Sun !—
The " Glory of" that " Lebanon ! "

HALLELUJAH!

Hallelujah! Hallelujah!
  Praise the Father! He is Love:
Hallelujah! let our voices
  Join with seraph choirs above.

Hallelujah! praise to Jesus!
  Sinners, crushed beneath your guilt,
Rise! rejoice! adore the Saviour!
  'Twas for you his blood was spilt.

Hallelujah! praise the Spirit!
  He doth sinful hearts renew;
Sanctifier, Guide, Consoler,
  Teacher, ever kind and true.

Hallelujah! swell the chorus,
  God, our only God adore!
To the Father, Son, and Spirit,
  Praise be now, and evermore.

DOXOLOGY.

"Glory be to the Father, and to the Son, and to the Holy Ghost! As it was in the beginning, is now, and ever shall be, world without end. Amen."

HALLELUJAH ! joyful raise
Heart and voice our God to praise !
Praise the Father! praise the Son!
Praise the Spirit! Three in One !
One in wisdom and in grace,
One to save our sinful race :
Triune God! to Thee be given
Praise on Earth, and praise in Heaven !

CAXTON PRINTING WORKS, CAMDEN ROAD, N.W.

BY THE SAME AUTHOR.

HOMEWARD BOUND AND OTHER
SERMONS.   Price 6s.

THE ANTIDOTE TO FEAR; with Illus-
trations from the Prophet Isaiah.   Cloth 2s. 6d. ;
gilt or red edges, 3s.

THE AUTHOR OF "THE SINNERS'
FRIEND."   An Autobiography, compiled from a
Diary, from 1810 to 1860, by Mr. J. VINE HALL,
Edited by his Son, the author of " Come to Jesus."
8s. 6d.

THE CHRISTIAN PHILOSOPHER
TRIUMPHING OVER DEATH.   4s.

www.ingramcontent.com/pod-product-compliance
Lightning Source LLC
Chambersburg PA
CBHW030613040726
47497CB00008B/2965